Life in Color

Life *in* Color

VT **VISUAL THERAPY'S**

Guide to the Perfect Palette—
for Fashion, Beauty, and You!

by Jesse Garza and Joe Lupo
Foreword by Rita Wilson

CHRONICLE BOOKS
SAN FRANCISCO

Pages 195 and 198 constitute a continuation of the copyright page.

Library of Congress Cataloging-in-Publication Data available.

ISBN: 978-0-8118-6523-4

Manufactured in China
Designed by Omnivore

10 9 8 7 6 5 4 3 2 1

Chronicle Books LLC
680 Second Street
San Francisco, California 94107

www.chroniclebooks.com

TO OUR CLIENTS:
OUR TRUE
INSPIRATION

Jesse A Garza

Joe Lupo

TABLE OF CONTENTS

FOREWORD

Color scares me.
When Jesse asked if I would write the foreword to his and Joe's new book, I replied, "What would a 'Whimsical/Chic/rockedout/Earth' who loves black and gray know about color?"

I told him I would think about it, since I was so busy sorting my black T-shirts by sleeve length, v-neck, scoop neck, Henley, crew neck, bedazzled, J.Crew, and designer. But being in the blanket of black T-shirts got me thinking. What happened? I used to wear color. I used to love color. I was a color person. In the '80s I wore a shocking pink taffeta Vicky Tiel gown with matching shoes and gloves to the Academy Awards. There was that acid green Yohji Yamamoto three-piece satin suit I wore to my tenth high school reunion. Somewhat recently, there was a turquoise Juicy Couture sweat suit I wore one summer, even though I did more eating than sweating in it. All this remembrance of raiments past made me nostalgic for something. I missed color. When I think back on my favorite dresses, so many of them were colorful. I loved bright floral prints more than I liked stripes or graphic prints. I liked color blocking, where one bright color was on top and another on the bottom. I used to layer two different colored T-shirts over a pair of jeans. A bright colored purse or scarf thrilled me. A coral necklace made me quiver. But there was also some uncertainty about color. I knew some colors looked better on me than others, but didn't quite know why. I knew yellow looked better on my blonde girlfriends while I looked like a fire hydrant in it. Lavender, which always looked so luscious on the hanger, made me look like last year's lilacs. On me, light greens, the color of doctor's scrubs, made me look as if I should be on a stretcher being rushed to the hospital. All the uncertainty of which colors actually looked good on me made wearing color too much of a gamble. Color was hard. It was easier to just wear what was safe. That's when I started the descent into darkness.

Even though I was finding it very comfortable in my blagreigebrown world, I loved seeing everyone else in color. I admired the confidence of women who would wear a red gown. Even though I am not a green person, I was secretly envious of women who could wear it. It made me blue to see women wearing blue, which, in my closet, would only appear in the form of jeans and the occasional navy sweater. I was wearing black but I was tangled up in the blues.

Black has its virtues, though. Black, as we all know, is chic. It is classic. It is safe. It is easy. It always looks clean. It is slimming. It goes with everything. It is easily identifiable. No one ever asks, "Hey, what do you call that color." There are no confusing euphemisms for it as there are for, say, maroon, as in aubergine or eggplant, or *melitzana*, which is Greek for aubergine. And how did "aubergine" get into the English lexicon anyway?

While we are on the subject of black, let me give a shout-out to white. White reflects light and can be bleached. As far as I'm concerned, white has no virtues. It is not good. Anyone who wears white is far too confident for my tastes. That person, with their bright, bleached, toothy grin, is shouting, "Ha! I mock you and your fear of dirt. Fie on stains! I look so perfect in white that I need not eat, drink, nor be merry! I will starve to achieve this look of perfection!" Yes, starve. Because there is not a woman alive who will put on a pair of white pants

and think her butt looks damn good in them. There will always be the fear that when you're checking your rear end out you will see a sticker on the three-way mirror that reads, "Caution: Items in this mirror are larger than they appear."

And white T-shirts! I am exhausted trying to find the perfect white T-shirt that doesn't cling, hits at the right length, isn't see-through, is the right thickness, doesn't have to be thrown away after three washings, and doesn't stretch out while you are wearing it. White is for doctors and brides, okay?

Okay. Fine. Maybe I'm being a bit harsh on white. All right. I confess. I actually love white. I love the way it reflects light on my face. I love the way white makes me look when it's summer and I have a slight fake tan. I love a white bathrobe after a shower. I do love white. But white doesn't love me as much as black does. Black is comfy. Black is good to me. What has black ever done to harm me? Black is black. That's why I am loyal to black. I am a monochromatic monogamist. Or am I?

Reminiscing about my bygone romances with color has awakened a desire in me to revisit the temptation of tint. It has been too long since I have lived without color in my clothes. Besides, I had some really good times with color. What's so scary? There really isn't anything to lose (except for a few pounds here and there). What's the worst that can happen? Some dog might mistake me for that hydrant? I can always go back to the safety of my neutrals. If I try color, no one is going to get hurt, except maybe that person who wears white and looks perfect all the time. So, I'm going

to go for it. I am going fearlessly into the wild blue yonder of spectrum. I am ready to ride the rainbow of risk to find that jackpot of goldenrod. It is time to come out of the shadows and into the light of color. Out of my way, beige. Fuchsia, here I come!

—Rita Wilson

INTRODUCTION

Let's face it: Color can either work for you or against you. As you make your grand entrance, you can bet people notice the way that drop-dead red dress brings out the rosiness in your cheeks—or, conversely, the way that dreary mustard yellow sweater makes you look drawn and worn. According to the Institute for Color Research, people make a subconscious judgment about a person, environment, or product within 90 seconds of initial viewing, and somewhere between 62 and 90 percent of this assessment is based on color alone.

Think of cinematic fashion moments that have taken your breath away: Nicole Kidman's red dress in *Moulin Rouge!,* Faye Dunaway's golden beige sweater in *Bonnie and Clyde,* and Keira Knightley's 1930s green gown in *Atonement.* All these looks make an impact largely because of color.

The colors you wear dictate how light reflects off your face, eyes, hair, and skin—so color can help make the most of who you are, or undermine your natural good looks. You've probably heard that lighting design determines how beautiful an actress looks on film. Well, you're the star of your own movie! Think of the colors you wear as your own personal light filters. Of course you'll want to choose the most flattering ones!

Black may have dominated fashionable closets for the past two decades, but the tide is turning back toward color. Grace Coddington, creative director of *Vogue* and self-confessed lifelong black addict, wore a bright green dress to the collections in Paris recently. "After 20 years of black, it seemed like the right time," she told *The New York Times.*

In our work as wardrobe consultants, we've learned that virtually every woman is intimidated by color. Since no one ever seems to be sure about which colors they should wear, most women choose to play it safe with a wardrobe of 100 percent blacks, darks, and neutrals. While this strategy won't land you on any worst-dressed lists, it won't win you any points for originality, either. And color-phobes miss out on the sheer joy that comes from putting something on that lights you up—literally.

In this book, we'll help you find your best colors—and convince you to wear them! How will we do this? By *not* forcing you into some Technicolor Dreamcoat that makes you want to hide in a corner. This is a color book for fashion-minded people. The last thing we want is to see any of our clients in a pink pantsuit. We want to help you build a wardrobe that has a strong neutral foundation, and then teach you to use colors to show it off.

We have a philosophy of dressing that we like to call Cake versus Frosting. The cake of your wardrobe—no matter what your style—should consist of a strong foundation of simple, well-constructed garments in neutral colors that flatter you. The frosting is where you add your personal signature, where bright pop-colors turn a blah outfit into a LOOK.

How will you discover these magical colors? First, you'll answer some questions about your natural coloring—this is to determine your Colortype and corresponding palette. (Your Colortype is one of four categories that take into account elements of your natural coloring in order to determine your best colors. We'll be digging into the Colortypes and their applications later in the book.) Then you'll explore your style and personality, which will help you further refine your palette and decide precisely how and where color will come into your wardrobe.

Along the way, we'll discuss the science and psychology of color. We'll meet some color gurus and try to learn from their magic. And we'll get some tips from beauty and lifestyle experts so you can bring color into all areas of your life—not just your wardrobe.

Why We Wrote This Book

Since 1995, we've worked as luxury lifestyle consultants—collaborating with private clients on a quest to present their most authentic selves. We work with clients from the inside out, helping them discover what they want to communicate with their style, and then creating a closet that reflects that message. We aim for timeless style, teaching clients how to incorporate trends in order to help them express who they are through their wardrobes. We believe that while trends are a dime a dozen, lifelong style is worth a million.

Once we decided to take our business beyond the closets of our private clients, it became our mission to demystify fashion for women whose homes we couldn't visit in person. We wanted to create a system to help people identify and articulate what looked good on them—something they could memorize and internalize so wardrobe confidence would become automatic. The first step in this process was coming up with the five Styletypes, which we discuss at length in our first book, *Nothing to Wear?*, and which you may discover for yourself, here, in chapter four. Identifying the Styletypes—essentially, fashion personalities—allowed us to create a shorthand in describing someone's style so that, with remarkable clarity, we'd be able to envision a woman's best looks just by hearing a few words about her. After determining a woman's Styletype, we immediately have an idea of who she is both inside and out, and which looks will suit her.

We take the "types" even further in this book. Making use of our years of experience with dressing women of all types, we formulated the system of Colortypes, four palettes designed to flatter women's different skin tone, hair, and eye color combinations. We've designed a simple quiz to help you discover which Colortype you are. You'll find the Colortype quiz in chapter two.

When we were young, our mothers—and everyone else's—carried around a book called *Color Me Beautiful* like a fashion bible. Carole Jackson's bestselling text provided the authority on color, grouping women into seasons and providing them with strict palettes from which to draw their wardrobe colors. Arming women with a clear set of rules, *Color Me Beautiful* gave millions the confidence to go shopping for vivid clothing and makeup.

In creating our Colortype system, we drew inspiration from Ms. Jackson's groundbreaking book, but we wanted to broaden women's options and encourage their creativity, so we came up with 20 Color- and Styletype combinations, instead of four seasons. We believe that, when incorporating color into her life, a woman needs to take not only her natural coloring into consideration, but also her style. No longer will redheads be confined to earth tones, and no longer will every woman of color be relegated to the same palette. In our system, a caramel-skinned Southeast Asian woman and a freckled Irish-American woman may indeed belong to the same Colortype.

Adding a woman's Colortype to what we like to call her "fashion dossier" creates a powerful store of information. Armed with this info, we not only know her taste but also her coloring—this way, we can pick out what suits her without a face-to-face meeting.

But this shorthand is not just for our benefit. To many women with lives reaching far beyond their closets, fashion can seem like a confusing sea—a churning jumble of leggings and tunics and bustiers, oh my! Flipping through fashion magazines makes many women feel alienated—*Who are these socialites, anyway?*—and they may opt out of fashion entirely, languishing in a wardrobe of chain-store coordinates.

We want fashion to make sense to all women, not just the boldface names on the coasts (though goodness knows, we love them, too!). We want to make it simple and easy to choose the best clothes by providing a clear, concise set of guidelines that guarantees a woman will only buy things that flatter her. What woman doesn't love a checklist? Once a lady knows her Styletype and Colortype, she is equipped with all the information she needs to hit the stores like a professional stylist. She'll need only to stick to the colors and silhouettes on her list to look put-together and confident.

To make shopping easy, we've included Pantone color chip stickers, so that after taking a few quizzes to determine her Color- and Styletype, a woman can assemble her very own, personalized palette, to take with her on-the-go. No longer will she hover over the sweater table, agonizing between lavender and periwinkle.

What happens when trends change, you ask? Fashion is a living, breathing organism—you can't trap it in a jar. The Styletypes are timeless, since they describe taste in shape, fabrication, and details, rather than silhouettes or hemlines. And we've included such a wide variety of shades on each of the Colortype palettes that every woman will be able to find her red, blue, purple, brown—even Day-Glo!—and participate in trends as they strike her fancy.

Our hope is that this book will take away fashion confusion, and encourage fashion creativity. When you're no longer afraid of making a horrible mistake with your wardrobe, you can make magic.

Color is to the eye
what music is to the ears
and *love to the heart.*

— Amy Fine Collins

CHAPTER 1
WHY COLOR MATTERS

When we see the colors we associate with childhood, we feel good. This effect explains the connection among colors, memories, and emotions—colors we associate with positive memories make us feel happy, and those we associate with negative memories make us feel sad. This may seem obvious, but most of us take this connection for granted. Think of it next time you have what seems like an irrationally negative reaction to a shade of bright purple—maybe it reminds you of that overbearing kindergarten teacher who humiliated you a million years ago, or a terrible *Barney & Friends* episode.

Perhaps "vivid" memories are so-called because they appear in color. Color plays an important role in our subconscious—both Freud and Jung considered it crucial to the interpretation of dreams.

Jesse's first memory of color is the glorious chaos of finger painting—the joy of making a mess. (He must have gotten all the mess-making out of his system at an early age, considering how fastidious he is now!)

Think back to the tactile bliss of finger painting: the fun of mashing a bunch of shades together and being surprised by the results. Children are attracted to all colors—we develop our specific preferences later in life.

Whenever you're feeling closed off to color, try to remember those days in kindergarten when you were open to it all—how happy color made you!—and approach your wardrobe with new eyes.

Joe's first color memory is of the pink terrycloth duck that went with him everywhere as a little boy. Oh, and his grandmother's green handbag. And wearing a red cowboy hat and nothing else while riding his rocking horse. As a kid, Joe had a red, white, and blue room—and a pink closet. He was born with a rainbow spoon in his mouth. Things haven't changed much for Joe.

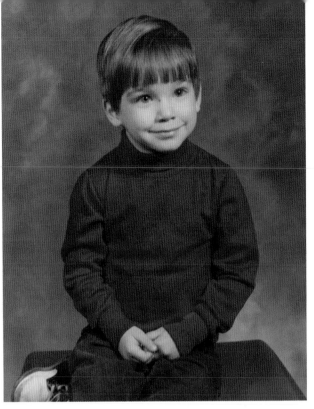

Even as a preschooler, Joe had a classic sense of color—notice the all-American navy and red combo he's wearing here, popped with the unexpected snap of classic saddle shoes. In retrospect, he wishes someone had thought to polish them.

Understanding your emotional associations with color can be a powerful tool to help ensure successful wardrobe-building. Here's a fun exercise: Pull out old family photos from your childhood, and take note of the colors that appear in your favorites. Finding a new sweater to match one your mom wore in the '70s can provide an unexpected mood boost and a sense of connection to your own personal history.

Here's Jesse with his sister and brother, a few years post–finger painting. Notice how he made sure to incorporate the red worn by his siblings into his plaid jacket. A master of coordination, even at eight years old!

Perhaps it's our love for the color aqua that brought us together. Jesse says it makes him feel enveloped in goodness and light; Joe says it reminds him of the beaches of the Caribbean. We both wear it when we want to project calm and confidence.

Color Attraction

It's not only memory that dictates our taste in color. Gender, culture, and age play major roles, too. A study done in 1897 concluded that women prefer red to blue, and men prefer blue to red, which certainly reflects our cultural associations with the two colors. (It's interesting to note that baby blue, a calm and peaceable color, was originally associated with girls, and baby pink, which packs more of a punch because of its strong red undertones, was associated with boys. No one seems to know when attitudes toward blue and pink shifted.) A recent study determined that women are more likely than men to have a favorite color, which is not surprising, considering men are more likely to be color blind. Next time your husband pairs a yellow shirt with an orange tie, respond compassionately—his taste might not be his fault!

Color and Culture

Colors have different meanings in different cultures—meanings that run so deep, they can actually dictate personal preferences. For example, white is the color of weddings in the United States, but in the Far East, it's the color of funerals. So if you're planning to get married in China, don't wear a white dress!

Here are some more examples of different ways different cultures view the color spectrum:

Red

Fertility— *Africa, China, New Guinea, India*
Protection—*Ancient Rome, Gypsies, Incan Empire, Kabbalists, Scotland*
The Hunt—*Brazil, Scandinavia*
War—*Ancient Rome, Ethiopia, Maori*
Honor—*Nigeria, United States, Western Europe*
Death—*Ancient Arabia, Philippines*
Luck—*Greece*
Brides—*China*

When in doubt, wear red. —*Bill Blass*

Orange

Happiness and Love—*China, Japan*
Kinship—*Native Americans*
Gluttony—*Christianity*

Orange is the happiest color. —*Frank Sinatra*

Yellow

Happiness—*United States*
Mourning—*Egypt*
Courage—*Japan*
Jealousy—*France*

What a horrible thing yellow is. —*Edgar Degas*

Green

Growth and Fertility—*Africa*
Health—*Egypt*
Luck—*China, Ireland*
Envy—*Ancient Greece*
Honor—*Scotland*

It's not easy being green. —*Kermit The Frog*

Blue

Preciousness—*Japan*
Love—*Western Africa*
Femininity—*Indonesia*
Fear—*Ancient Rome*
Mourning—*Ancient Turkey*
Despair—*India*
Purity—*Catholicism*
Peace—*United Nations*
Sadness—*United States*
Truth, Faith, and Loyalty—*Medieval Europe*
Respectability—*Great Britain*
Immortality—*China*
Paradise—*Iran*
Mourning—*Mexico*

I never get tired of the blue sky. —*Vincent van Gogh*

Tone Trivia: *Cleopatra* loved the color purple and had her servants soak 20,000 Purpura snails for more than a week to get an ounce of purple dye.

22

White

Mourning—*China*
Wedding—*Western World*
Cleanliness—*Western World*
Good Dreams—*Ancient Greece*

The first of all single colors is white... We shall set down white for the representative of light, without which no color can be seen; yellow for the earth; green for water; blue for air; red for fire; and black for total darkness. —*Leonardo da Vinci*

Gray

Lent—*Christianity*

Better gray than garishness.
—*Jean-Auguste-Dominique Ingres*

Brown

Mourning—*India*
Self-discipline—*Native Americans*

I cannot pretend to feel impartial about colors. I rejoice with the brilliant ones and am genuinely sorry for the poor browns. —*Winston Churchill*

Black

Mourning—*Western World*
War—*Aztecs*

There's something about black. You feel hidden away in it. —*Georgia O'Keeffe*

Pink

Wealth—*Namibia*
Masculinity—*Japan*
Joy—*Catholicism*

Pink is the navy blue of India. —*Diana Vreeland*

Purple

Nobility—*Ancient Rome, Byzantine Empire—
and most other Western civilizations*
Celebration—*Ancient Greece*
Mourning—*Thailand*
Wisdom, Gratitude, and Healing—*Native Americans*
Wealth—*Japan*
Faith—*Egypt*

I think it pisses God off if you walk by the color purple in a field somewhere and don't notice it.
—*Alice Walker*

THE SCIENCE OF COLOR

In visual perception, a color is almost never seen as it really is—as it physically is. This fact makes color the most relative medium in art. —Josef Albers, *world-renowned artist, Yale professor, and color expert*

LET'S START THINKING ABOUT COLOR BY DEFINING IT EXACTLY. FIRST AND FOREMOST, COLOR IS A PERCEPTION—A PRODUCT OF HOW OUR BRAINS PROCESS LIGHT WAVES BOUNCING OFF OBJECTS. THEREFORE, COLOR IS TOTALLY SUBJECTIVE.

This subjective element is probably why opinions of color are so diverse, sometimes even controversial. Since no two people experience the same color the same way—our brain mediates our perception of every color we see—no two people can feel the same way about color.

Light waves enable us to see. These waves are made up of every color in the spectrum—remember ROY G. BIV from second-grade science?—and the colors we see are determined by which light waves a particular object absorbs, versus those it reflects. This all sounds crazily complicated, but it's not.

We think of pure light as white, right? That's because when light is shining into the air, there's nothing solid to absorb its waves, and the combination of all the colors in the spectrum produces the color we think of as white.

Our eyes can see just a small percentage of the waves contained in the electromagnetic spectrum. On one side of this small spectrum are blue wavelengths, which are relatively short, and on the opposite side are red wavelengths, which are relatively long. All the colors of the rainbow fall in between red and blue. White is all the color wavelengths combined, while black is the absence of light, and so the absence of color.

Objects appear to be whichever color they are because they absorb some of the wavelengths contained in white light and reflect the rest. For example, a green dress absorbs all the wavelengths except green, a red dress absorbs all the wavelengths except red, and a black dress absorbs all the wavelengths. A white dress, it follows, reflects all the wavelengths and absorbs none.

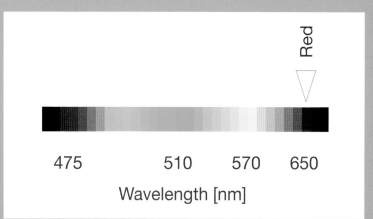

Light waves are just part of the experience of color. The other part of the experience occurs in our eyes and brains, where we process the information the light waves give us. Our retinas contain light sensors called rods and cones. Rods give us a coloring-book outline of the world, and cones are the crayons that enable our brains to fill in the colors. (There are three kinds of cones, allowing us to see different wavelengths of light.) Our brain then synthesizes all the information our retinas provide to produce a complete, colored-in image.

All this technical information is interesting, but it doesn't explain the pure, emotional experience of color—its ability to bring back memories, affect mood, and make an impression.

Color is an inborn gift, but appreciation of value is merely training of the eye, which everyone ought to be able to acquire. —John Singer Sargent, *artist*

ANIMALS AND COLOR

EXAMINING COLOR PERCEPTION REVEALS THAT ALL CREATURES SEE THE WORLD IN THEIR OWN WAY.

Things appear differently depending on who's seeing them, because the color of an object is dictated by the nervous system of the animal seeing it. It follows, then, that humans and other animals see color differently. Dogs have a sepia filter, so the world looks to them like an old photograph, which might explain their sweet and sentimental nature. Cats, on the other hand, have a blue filter, which enables them to see in the dark (sneaky!). Birds see the broadest range of color of all animals—ultraviolet light is visible to them—so birds that appear neutral and nondescript to humans might actually be the dandiest of their flocks.

WHAT IS SATURATION?

THOSE WHO WORK WITH FABRICS USE THE TERM "SATURATION" TO DESCRIBE A COLOR'S DEPTH AND INTENSITY. TECHNICALLY SPEAKING, SATURATION IS A MEASURE OF A COLOR'S PURITY. A HIGHLY SATURATED COLOR CONTAINS A VERY NARROW SCOPE OF WAVE-LENGTHS, SO IT APPEARS MORE INTENSE THAN A LESS SATURATED VERSION OF THE SAME HUE.

Pale Pink   Hot Pink

The Color Wheel

No matter which meanings they assign to colors, most cultures use one visual aid to illustrate colors' relation-ships to one another. Surely you've seen some version of the color wheel—a tool used mostly by artists in determining color harmonies and explaining how to mix hues. The first color wheel was developed more than 300 years ago, in 1666, by Sir Isaac Newton.

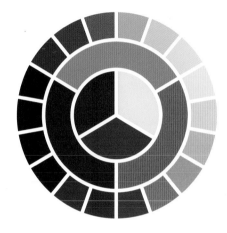

You probably already know that the founda-tion of the color wheel includes the three primary colors—red, yellow, and blue. The primary colors deserve their VIP status because they contain all the pigments necessary to create any other color of the rainbow (with the exception of black or white, of course).

The next part of the color wheel contains the secondary colors—green, orange, and purple—which can be mixed from the primary colors.

Finally, the tertiary colors—the third level on the color wheel—are mixed by combining one primary and one secondary color (e.g., yellow-orange and blue-green).

We won't concern ourselves much with the specifics of the color wheel—it's too technical for what we're doing here. (Don't worry, we're not going to have you mixing RIT dyes in your washing machine.)

However, the color wheel is useful when learning to combine colors harmoniously in an outfit.

Put simply, color harmony is the state of two or more colors looking good together. *Good* is subjective, of course, but for our purposes, it applies to an outfit that appears neither too loud nor too boring. As a rule, *complementary colors*—those directly across from one another on the color wheel—make nice duos.

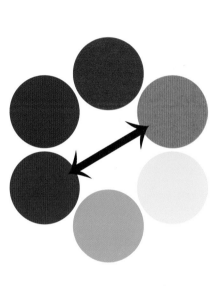

Complementary colors orange and blue stole the show at Jil Sander's Spring 2008 presentation.

Analogous colors—those side by side on a 12-part color wheel—also complement one another beautifully.

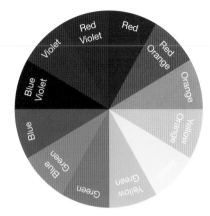

This look from Louis Vuitton's Spring 2008 collection is demure and elegant, but still joyous because of its use of analogous colors. When you hear someone use the word tonal to describe an outfit's color scheme, they are referring to looks like this one.

Dressing tonally is a great way to combine elements of your wardrobe that don't "match." Wearing a variety of shades of the same color at once conveys sophistication, richness, and, when the colors are vibrant, a creative sense of whimsy. For example, imagine a pair of navy pants with a midnight blue T-shirt and a superfine cardigan in baby blue, popped with a sapphire cocktail ring. Or, try opaque tights in deep brown with a khaki shirtdress and brown riding boots.

Now that you know a bit about color theory and history, it's time to translate that knowledge to your wardrobe. Color is a language, and just like Italian or French, it's not enough to read—you must put your new language into practice. In the next chapter, you'll discover your best colors.

Our good friend Patrick McDonald, who we know from the New York fashion scene, inspires style mavens with his peacock-like sensibility.

I consider myself a dandy artist. In the morning I am a blank canvas, and my color is not paint, but clothing.

Color is a statement. I'm not shy to say I like making a statement. It's very thought-out. Even though some people have thought things I've worn have been over the top, if you pull apart everything, it all makes sense together.

My mother took my brother and me to the Pucci palace in Florence when we were 12 years old. My mother bought 11 dresses and we met Emilio Pucci. All the colors and prints overwhelmed me in a positive, enchanted fashion way.

I was really fascinated by all the bright colors of the glam rock movement—when I came to LA for college, I went to Fred Segal on Santa Monica Boulevard, where Elton John shopped, and I bought electric blue ostrich platform shoes.

Things are getting more colorful in fashion these days. I'm so excited to see the end of this gray prisoner/warden uniform look. For a long time in men's fashion, you'd get

I have a guy who makes all my hats—Rod Keenan—and at the beginning of each season I bring him swatches of everything I'm wearing and he makes me hats to match.

excited seeing one piece of purple. Now people are more daring.

I love the movie *Velvet Goldmine*. That was the beginning of me being free in my head, thinking, "This is me. This is what I'm going to do. If people don't like it, I don't care. I was so happy in my own skin—finally."

I have worn all black in certain circumstances—when I'm feeling Gothic, or in a dark mood.

I do adore a rock-and-roll sensibility. I try to incorporate a bit of glam rock, King's Road, and Vivienne Westwood into my look.

The best color in the whole world is the one that looks good *on you!*

— Coco Chanel

CHAPTER 2
THE SYSTEM AND THE QUIZ

Now that you've learned a bit about color, it's time to figure out which ones are right for you. Let's move from theory to practice—practice wearing colors that make you come alive.

Over the two decades we've been working with clients, we've found the anxiety-inducing element of building a wardrobe is not tummy-minimizing or bust-maximizing, but choosing and incorporating color.

Why are we all so afraid to wear color? Is it that we don't want to draw attention to ourselves? Have we all come to believe that looking "just okay" in black is better than risking a fashion faux pas in bright red, or blue, or purple? There's something to this fear, of course. No one wants to show up to an important event looking like Violet, that greedy blueberry girl from *Charlie and the Chocolate Factory*.

But, thank goodness, we don't live our lives in black and white. Imagine how boring that would be! So why should we live our fashion lives that way?

Tone Trivia: *A psychologist* specializing in the meaning of color found that narcissists' favorite color is commonly blue-green.

The rainbow spectrum may seem overwhelmingly broad, but with our system it's easy to narrow down to just those hues that flatter your individual coloring.

The most important thing about discovering your Colortype? You must approach the process with an open mind. Be prepared to let go of preconceived notions of which colors look best on you. Maybe, when you were twentysomething, the lady at the cosmetics counter told you that red was your color. Well, that's not necessarily the case anymore. Coloring and taste change as we go through different stages in our lives, and our best colors change too. This system is all about your coloring NOW.

By analyzing our clients' hair, skin, and eye colors—as well as the garments they've come to love and loathe—we help them choose personalized palettes for their wardrobes. Our system is quick and foolproof, and now we're pleased to share it with you.

In creating our color-matching formula, we took inspiration from the skies. The solar system has been a source of fascination and wonder for people all over the world since ancient times. From the glorious, pulsing heat of the Sun to the cool radiance of the Moon, and from the rich green of the Earth to the incandescent glow of the stars, celestial bodies lend themselves beautifully to inspiring the four palettes of colors you'll choose from.

We've separated women into four Colortypes, directly inspired by the four kinds of "glow" emitted by these glorious orbs: the Sun, the Moon, the Earth, and the stars.

Chances are, you know intuitively which kind of heavenly body you are. Do you love the warm yellows and reds of the Sun or the soft blues and grays of the Moon? The rich greens, auburns, and browns of the Earth or the luminescent whites, magentas, and turquoises of the stars? Think, also, about the quality of light each of these bodies produces: the Moon's hazy glow, the clear brightness of the Sun, the soft reflection and warmth of the Earth, the shimmering twinkle of the stars. Which of these kinds of light would you look best in?

Color is something that either feels right or doesn't. When we follow our instincts, it's hard to go wrong.

But just in case you don't trust your instincts yet, we've come up with this quick and easy quiz to help you determine which Colortype you are.

Quiz: Which Colortype Are You?

For each question below, circle the answer that best applies to you. If you're torn between two answers, circle both of them. Our scoring process allows for multiple answers in order to give you a totally personalized palette. We've done our best to include a wide range of eye, skin, and hair colors, but everyone's coloring is unique, so choose the closest match you see here.

1. Which one of these most closely resembles your eye color?

Note: No printed colors can truly reflect the multifaceted hues of the iris. Choose the closest match.

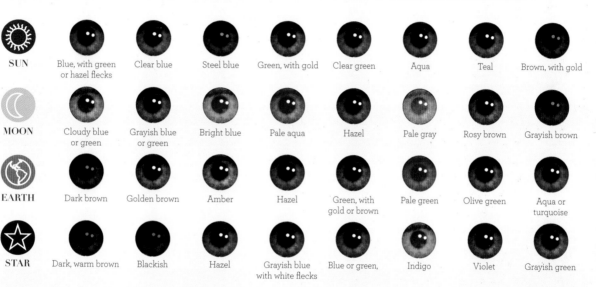

SUN	Blue, with green or hazel flecks	Clear blue	Steel blue	Green, with gold	Clear green	Aqua	Teal	Brown, with gold
MOON	Cloudy blue or green	Grayish blue or green	Bright blue	Pale aqua	Hazel	Pale gray	Rosy brown	Grayish brown
EARTH	Dark brown	Golden brown	Amber	Hazel	Green, with gold or brown	Pale green	Olive green	Aqua or turquoise / Teal blue
STAR	Dark, warm brown	Blackish	Hazel	Grayish blue with white flecks	Blue or green,	Indigo	Violet	Grayish green

2. Which one of these most closely resembles your skin color?

 SUN: Your skin is warm with tawny, peachy, or golden undertones. In the sun, you tan and freckle. You blush peach. Your skin color ranges from creamy to freckly; tawny to caramel.

Famous Suns: Kristen Bell, Sarah Jessica Parker, Katie Couric, Tyra Banks.

 MOON: Your skin is cool with blue or pink undertones. Moons can be ultra-pale or dusky dark. If you're ultra-pale you probably don't tan, but if you do, you burn first. Your skin may have a translucent quality. Your skin color ranges from ivory to rose; beige to light mocha.

Famous Moons: Sharon Stone, Marcia Cross, Cate Blanchett, Bai Ling.

 EARTH: Your skin is warm with golden or terra-cotta under-tones. You can develop a deep tan in the sun, but without sun exposure, you may be pale with little or no cheek color. Your skin color ranges from fair to bronze to brown.

Famous Earths: Teri Hatcher, Susan Sarandon, Alicia Keys, Kerry Washington.

 STAR: Your skin is cool, or olive, with blue undertones. Stars run the spectrum from palest pale to deepest brown-black. If you are an alabaster Star you rarely tan and tend to burn, but if you are a deeper toned Star you tan and rarely burn. Regardless, you tend not to freckle. Your skin color ranges from alabaster to pearl, deep olive to espresso.

Famous Stars: Gwen Stefani, Courtney Cox Arquette, Salma Hayek, Michelle Obama.

3. Which one of these most closely resembles the color your skin turns when you blush?

 SUN — Rose, Dusty coral

 EARTH — Deep warm brown, Overripe peach, Rich pinkish coral

 MOON — Bright pink, Rose pink

 STAR — No color, Dusty rose, Purplish, Intense blood red

4. Which one of these most closely resembles your current hair color (natural or chemically treated)?
Note: No printed colors can truly reflect the various shades in our hair. Choose the closest match.

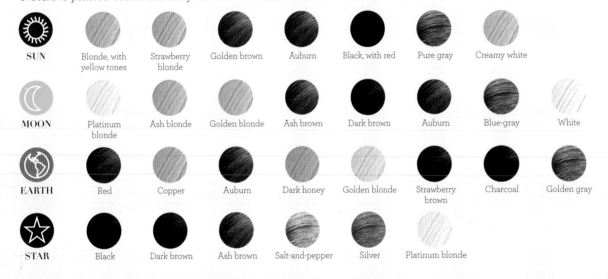

SUN	Blonde, with yellow tones	Strawberry blonde	Golden brown	Auburn	Black, with red	Pure gray	Creamy white
MOON	Platinum blonde	Ash blonde	Golden blonde	Ash brown	Dark brown	Auburn	Blue-gray	White
EARTH	Red	Copper	Auburn	Dark honey	Golden blonde	Strawberry brown	Charcoal	Golden gray
STAR	Black	Dark brown	Ash brown	Salt-and-pepper	Silver	Platinum blonde

5. Would you describe your coloring as warm or cool? (See "Are You Warm or Cool?" if you don't know.)

 SUN Warm

 MOON Cool

 EARTH Warm

STAR Cool

6. Which of the colors below is closest to the color of your favorite sweater or T-shirt?

SUN	Golden yellow	Safari brown	Peony pink	Ripe peach	Dusty purple	Apple green	Sky blue
MOON	Bright, sunny yellow	Kelly green	Teal blue	Cobalt blue	Fuchsia pink	True violet	Charcoal gray
EARTH	Tangerine orange	Brick red	Rich eggplant	Dark teal green	Dark khaki	Burgundy	Chocolate
STAR	Black	Ruby red	Sapphire blue	Lemon yellow	Icy pink	Icy blue	True white

ARE YOU WARM OR COOL?

YOU'LL OFTEN HEAR COLOR EXPERTS—FASHION DESIGNERS, MAKEUP ARTISTS, HAIRDRESSERS—REFERRING TO THE CONCEPTS OF WARM AND COOL. IN TERMS OF MAKEUP OR CLOTHING COLORS, WARM TENDS TO MEAN REDS, PINKS, AND ORANGES, WHILE COOL CONNOTES BLUES, GREENS, AND PURPLES. BUT PEOPLE'S SKIN TONES CAN BE WARM OR COOL, TOO, AND THIS IS WHERE THINGS CAN GET CONFUSING. IN SKIN-TONE TERMS, WARM REFERS NOT TO RED BUT TO GOLDEN. HERE'S HOW TO DISCERN WHICH CATEGORY YOU FALL INTO:

Stand near a large window at midday. Use a hand mirror to examine the area beneath your eyes. Is it: deep blue/purple (cool), or yellow/green/brown (warm)?

Hold a piece of white paper next to your cheek. In contrast to the pure white, does your cheek appear to have a blue/pink cast (cool), or a yellow/orange one (warm)?

Look at the roots of your hair. Are they:
Golden (warm)
Reddish (warm)
Ash gray or blonde (cool)
Blue-black (cool)
Brown with red highlights (warm)
Brown with blonde highlights (cool)

Look at the veins on your inner wrist. Are they:
Yellow/green (warm)
Blue/Gray (cool)

Most people will fall clearly into one category or the other. The exceptions are those with true olive skin, which can be mistaken as warm, but is actually cool. If you fall into this territory, hold a pair of khaki pants, then a white T-shirt, up to your face. If the khaki flatters you, you're probably warm. If you prefer the stark white, you're likely cool. If you're cool, you're likely a Moon or Star. If you're warm, you're likely a Sun or Earth.

7. Which of the groups of colors below do you feel would look very unflattering on you?

 SUN
 Bright red
Magenta
Royal blue
Bright orange

 EARTH
Blue-based pink
Bright purple
Soft lilac

 MOON
Mustard yellow
Burnt orange
Lime green

 STAR
Heathered-oatmeal beige
Warm peach
Heather green

8. If you were going to a fancy event, which of these would you wear?

 SUN
Beige-gold satin

 EARTH Dark teal green shantung

 MOON
Tiffany blue taffeta

 STAR
True red silk

9. Which of these colors is closest to your favorite lipstick?

 SUN
Sheer glossy peach

 EARTH
Deep brownish red

 MOON
True pink

 STAR
True blue-toned red

10. In which of these eye shadows would you not be caught dead?

 **SUN**
Blue

 EARTH
Sparkly white

 MOON
Deep brown

 STAR
Khaki

11. Which of these famous women share your coloring?

 Mischa Barton, Jada Pinkett Smith, Gisele Bündchen, Jennifer Aniston Vanessa Williams, Jade Jagger

 Gwyneth Paltrow, Naomi Watts, Nicole Kidman, Lucy Liu, Lena Horne

 Julianne Moore, Jennifer Lopez, Julia Roberts, Oprah Winfrey, Rosario Dawson, Eva Mendes

 Jennifer Connelly, Liv Tyler, Alek Wek, Gwen Stefani, Padma Lakshmi

Now that you've completed the quiz, count the number of each icon you have circled in order to determine your primary and secondary Colortypes.

The icon you have circled most frequently is your primary Colortype. The second most frequently circled icon is your secondary Colortype.

All the colors in your primary Colortype will flatter you. Consider your primary palette to be foolproof—you should be able to hand a sales associate your palette and let them pick out garments in any of the colors on it.

The colors in your secondary Colortype should be selected on an individual basis and are yours to pick and choose at your own discretion. We'll explain how to know whether a color looks good next to your skin in "Testing Your Results."

Note: Unlike some older philosophies of color selection, ours deems black universally flattering. Sure, black may not be the most interesting color, but the rumors are true: It will make you look skinnier, and it provides a neutral canvas for showcasing interesting jewelry or a great pair of shoes.

Before you say, "But I look terrible in yellow!" remember that, by embarking on this process, you've agreed to approach yourself with new eyes. Don't be afraid to try all the colors on your new palette. It's possible that what looks best on you may be a major departure from what you're used to wearing. It's okay to be apprehensive, but if you jump in with both feet, you'll be amazed by the change you see in yourself, both inside and out.

Testing Your Results

Once you've found your colors, it's important to double-check that they suit you. We know what you're thinking—*If I knew which colors suited me, I wouldn't need this book!* Well, don't worry; we're going to walk you through it.

Go back to the mirror. Look at the palette in your primary Colortype and find a garment in your base color. (The base color provides a foundation for each of the Colortype schemes. See page 46 for Sun, page 52 for Moon, page 58 for Earth, and page 64 for Star.) Bunch up the fabric like an elegant scarf—yes, you could even do this with an old T-shirt—and then arrange the garment next to your face. Look at yourself, and ask these questions:

Do my eyes pop? Do they look bigger and more intense, or tired?

Does my skin glow? (It should look healthy and vibrant. The wrong color brings out flaws and signs of aging, such as broken capillaries and under-eye circles; the right color seems to make them disappear.)

Does my hair look shiny and healthy? (Even if you color it, the color should look natural alongside a flattering garment.)

Most important, how do I feel? Am I comfortable? Do I like what I see in the mirror?

If you answer "no" to any of these questions, try testing the hues in your secondary Colortype. They may actually belong in first place. It's also important to note that not every single color in your palette will make your complexion sing. Play around to see what works best.

And now, without further ado, drum roll please . . . *take a look at your palette!* ➡

SUN

From peach to lemon, strawberry to mango, and lime to blueberry, shades on the sun palette are as refreshing as summer sorbet. Suns are golden girls—so they can wear tropical colors all year-round.

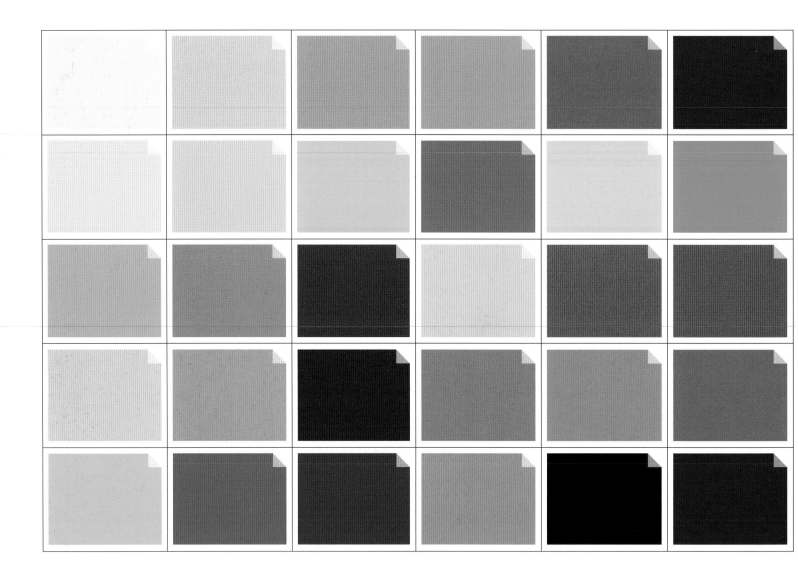

MOON

Moon women can't go wrong playing it cool—they're most gorgeous when they have the blues, from turquoise to slate, sky to Tiffany. Their cool skin tones will glow in contrast to blue-reds and pinks, from fuchsia to magenta, rose to petal.

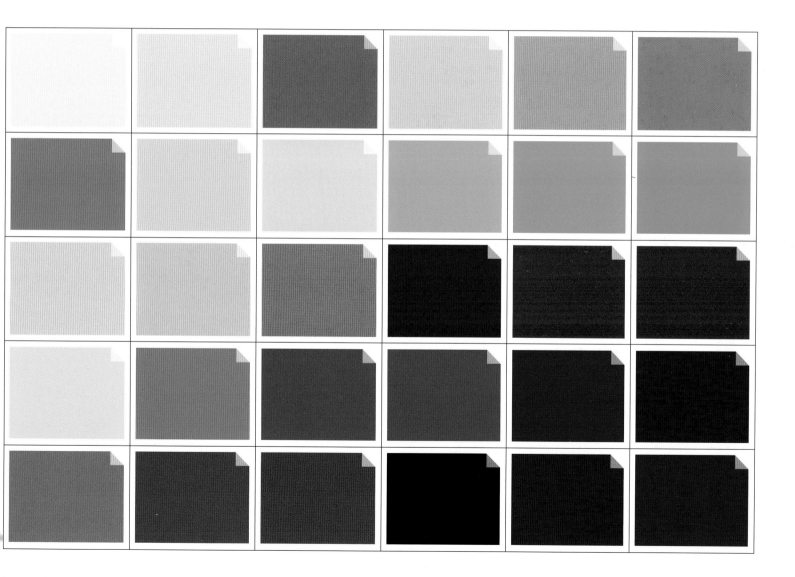

EARTH

All the sumptuous colors on the earth palette can be found
in the fairy tale forest, from ripe shades of berry and plum, to
rich moss greens and browns, to bright and cheery marigold,
peony, and lilac.

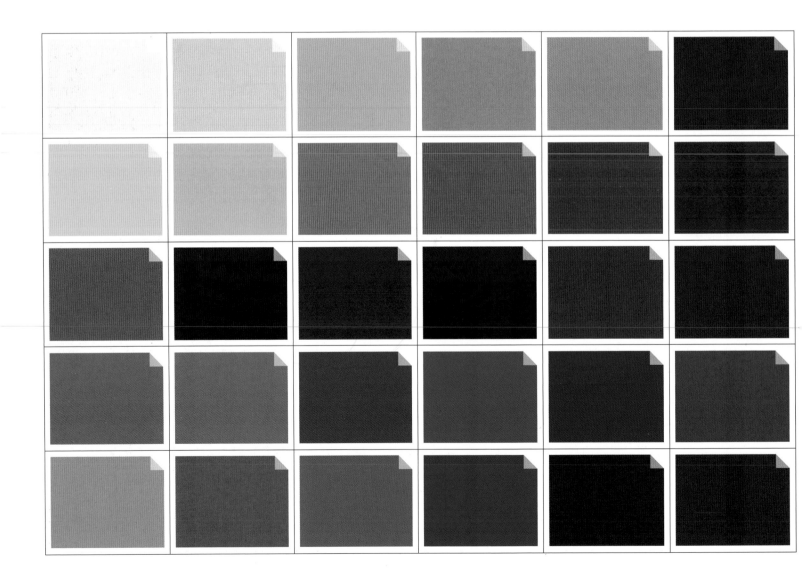

STAR

The Star comes out at night—and so do her best colors. Her palette is a wealth of modern jewel tones, from luminescent pearl to rarest emerald, ruby red to deep lapis blue.

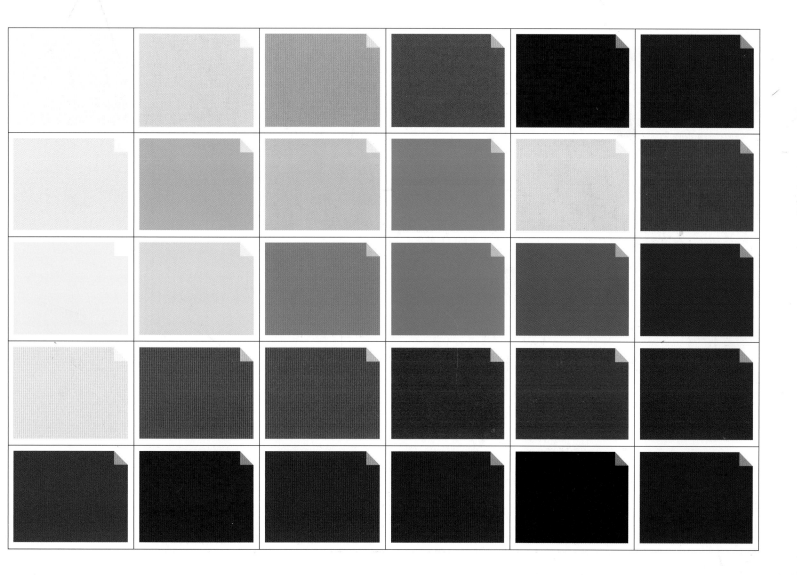

COLORTYPE: **Star**   STYLETYPE: **Chic**

SPRING/SUMMER SIGNATURE COLOR: **Aqua**

FALL/WINTER SIGNATURE COLOR: **Midnight Blue**

Here I am with a chocolate cake my mother made me for my birthday. I think it's true about loving colors you associate with good memories because I'm wearing midnight in this photo, at age 12, and I still feel best in it, at 43.

When I went into Ultimo (the most glamorous boutique in Chicago back in the day) for my job interview in the late 1980s, I had Flock of Seagulls hair, white pants, navy blue Byblos blazer—very Ricardo Montalban. You! Look! Mahvelous!

Joan Weinstein, the owner of Ultimo and the empress of Chicago fashion, loved the fact that my parents were missionaries—she knew I would be honest and hardworking. She said, "Cut the hair and put some black on and you'll be fine." We all wanted to fit in and be fashionistas.

Early '90s was Jil Sander/Armani somber. I was in my early 20s then. Wearing Armani had a big influence on my style—it provided me with a monochromatic uniform. Because Ultimo was a high-fashion store, one of the amazing perks was that at the end of the season we were allowed to buy pieces at a great discount.

Working with clients at Ultimo, I would be in a Jean-Paul Gaultier contraption one day, an architectural Claude Montana jacket the next. I would offset the avant-garde looks with Armani and Jil Sander, which were very clean and neutral. Joan wanted all her employees to practice what they preached, and the aesthetic we sold to clients was clean and modern.

The color palette was very neutral for me, and that's what I was attracted to. Joan pushed us all into that as a uniform—how could you look bad if you're wearing all black? I had really severe slicked-back hair, and the lines of my clothing were architectural.

The end result was that I and everyone else were perceived as the Addams family—we were chic, but people thought we were out of our minds.

Here I am with one of my gorgeous sisters in my New York uniform. Take the jacket off and I'm set for LA. It only took me 15 years to master bicoastal dressing!

When I turned 30 and decided to move to New York, I had rock-and-roll hair and wore long underwear T-shirts and Chrome Hearts!—I'm such a minimalist now that it's hard to believe I ever dressed like that.

When we got our business going in New York, I wanted to start a new phase of my life and be perceived differently. Joe and I did some consulting for Oxxford clothes, a pretty conservative, high-end brand. I cut my hair and jumped into pinstripe suits in order to get down to business.

After my business was established, I felt like I could get out of

My mother influenced me with her chic, monochromatic glamour and encouraged me from an early age to embrace my artistic side. Is style genetic? Look at her in her giraffe-tan striking a pose in a family photo. No wonder…

that. In your early 30s dressing conservative is cute, but in your mid-30s it starts to look like old banker guy. Around 35, I moved to LA part-time—and clothes that I wore all the time in New York didn't work there. I started wearing cargos and flip-flops, trying to seem nonchalant, yet I ended up spending more time getting dressed than if I had worn a suit. At times I'd go conservative and grab a polo shirt—I was lost. It took me a while to get into a groove.

Being relaxed-looking didn't really work for me. I felt I couldn't be "on" as a stylist. I wanted to represent the direction I was giving people. I took on jeans as a trademark and went for beautiful shoes, beautiful belts, a collared shirt, and a Tom Ford jacket. That's still my uniform. Remember, I'm doing closets and wardrobes, not mergers and acquisitions.

Looking back at all this, it wasn't really about the clothes. It was about how I wanted to be perceived throughout the different phases of my life. Now that I am working with clients and writing books, I finally know why I am here—not necessarily to be a stylist, but to be an inspiration.

This is me with my friend Anita. If you only knew how high my hair really was! Luckily, it disappears into the background a bit. Notice how I matched my red logo to hers — in the '80s, friends did things like that for one another.

Aqua is my number-one "pop" color. It is who I am and what I represent.

Here I am communing with nature — creator of more beautiful palettes than the most genius artist or designer. While sleeveless is entirely appropriate on vacation, please don't wear such a silhouette within city limits — it's Abercrombie and Forty. Notice the similarities between this photo and the one of me at age 12 — it's the same face, and the same feeling. Whether it's my mother's chocolate cake or the smell of lavender, I wear midnight during my happiest moments.

CHAPTER 3
THE COLORTYPES

Now that we've given you a taste of your colors, it's time to see them in action. Check out the women on the following pages in their wrong and right colors, and witness the power of the right-color T-shirt to bring hair, skin, and eyes to life.

You'll notice that the women in each Colortype don't look alike—there's diversity in skin, hair, and eye colors—even within the same categories. That's because we live in a world where race and ethnicity have blended together to create an infinite number of gorgeous permutations. There is no one-color-fits-all. Women who look very different from one another may actually share the same best colors.

SUN

Your palette is inspired by the golden light of the Sun—a force that illuminates and reveals the world's warm sparkle.

Your eyes
are likely a light color—blue, light brown, green, gray, or hazel—flecked with gold around the centers.

Your skin
is creamy or tawny, with a peachy or rosy undertone. You may be lucky enough to have freckles. In the sun, you grow burnished and golden.

Your hair
is a warm shade of mahogany, brown, blonde, or red. If you have highlights, they are redwood, golden, or strawberry-blonde. If your hair is very curly, it may have a burgundy or brick red cast when it catches the sun.

Icons of the Sun Colortype
include Glenn Close, Helen Mirren, Gisele Bündchen, Gayle King, and Nicole Richie.

Your best colors:
Yellows, corals, dusty roses

Your worst colors:
Bright pinks, blue-reds

Base color:
Rich saffron yellow

48

Loretta is the ultimate Sun. Her skin is warm and lightly tanned; her hair is naturally blonde. As she's matured, her hair has gotten lighter and become more ash blonde than golden. The natural sheen of her lips is peachy, and her eyes are green.

Like many blondes, Loretta has been told she looks great in white, but she can never seem to find the right white T-shirt. That's because white's iciness does little to emphasize Loretta's vibrant skin and sparkling eyes; in fact, its harshness emphasizes fine lines on her face. It also brings out the brassy yellow in her platinum hair.

← This ecru dress is just a few shades away from the white shirt, but it's worlds away in terms of how it flatters her. Because it has warm undertones instead of cool ones, it enhances Loretta's coloring. Almost magically, she looks younger.

What a Peach!

Even though Kim has a slightly deeper skin tone than Loretta—and dark brunette hair—she is also a classic Sun. Notice the way her natural flush is peachy, not red?

Kim thought gray would serve as a nice alternative to the black she wears every day. But this gray top draws out the sallow areas in her skin and makes her undertones appear more purplish than peachy. The shadows on her face—instead of her exquisite bone structure—are exaggerated.

➡ Reflected off this coral top, Kim's skin looks peachy, and her hair color appears richer. And listen up: Just because a girl is a size 14 or larger doesn't mean she has to cloak her body in dark colors! This top flatters Kim's body type as well as her coloring because of its deep-V placket, which draws attention to her bust area, and its longer length, which covers her tummy. And its brilliant coral color lights up her face and décolletage.

What a Gem!

Pale by Comparison

Even though deep saffron yellow is the Sun Colortype's base color, light yellow has too much white in it to flatter women with golden coloring. Notice how this light yellow shirt seems to disappear into Emily—or, rather, she disappears into it. Emily is a warm redhead rather than a cool one because her eyes are green, not blue, and her freckles are a warm brown. All these elements make her an iconic redheaded Sun.

← Next to this shade of green, Emily's hair appears bright, and her skin tone is invigorated—not to mention her eyes, the color of which deepens with the reflection of this green top. You may be thinking, "Do they actually expect me to wear such a bright shade of green head to toe?" Of course not! (Except to yoga class, or to bed.) But we hope Emily's look inspires you to try a touch of this color—whether in a T-shirt, a scarf, or a flirty dress.

Sunny Delight!

Rachal's undertones are a warm yellow and her hair has a reddish cast, which is why she is a Sun. This icy pink top lends a cold, bluish cast to her lips and makes her eyes seem tired.

➡ Sunny yellow, on the other hand, fires her up! Her teeth shine and her cheeks take on an instant flush. Isn't it amazing to see the warm apricot tones come out in her complexion when she's wearing the right color?

MOON

Your palette is inspired by the soft, cool glow of the Moon. Its calming blue light creates a soft luminescence, like the radiance of your skin.

Your eyes
may be blue-gray, without any gold, brown or green flecks, or dark gray, brown, or taupe with a black line around the iris.

Your skin
is pale and translucent, with blue and pink undertones. If you tan at all, you burn first, and then your skin turns brick red, not bronze.

Your hair
Ranges from dark ash brown to ash blonde, or an almost pinkish red. Your natural highlights are pale and buttery.

Icons of the Moon Colortype
include Blythe Danner, Keri Russell, Lena Horne, and Lucy Liu.

Your best colors:
Royal blue, ripe strawberry

Your worst colors:
Mustard yellow, bright orange

Base color:
Sky blue

54

Colleen is what we call a "cool redhead." Her skin is pink, not golden, and when her skin freckles, it also burns. Her hair is a deep auburn with dark mahogany lowlights.

Here, Colleen disproves the maxim that redheads always look good in green. Notice how her skin appears pink in comparison to the warm redness of her hair. This is a good clue to the fact that she'll look better in pinks and blues than greens and peaches.

⬅ See how Colleen's skin appears invigorated when she wears this light aqua dress? The dress flatters her because it represents a tone present in her eyes. The clear brightness of this shade is a signature of the Moon palette—Moons should stay away from anything dusty or warm and opt for the clear and cool.

Muddled

Carrie is a fair ash blonde. Her icy blue eyes and light hair make her a quintessential Moon, but because she applies self-tanner every day, her skin has taken on a false yellowness, when her undertones are really pink. This beige top magnifies the areas where Carrie didn't apply self-tanner. In these areas, her skin appears blue and sallow in contrast to the warmth of the faux bronze.

➡ Pale pink, though, brings out the rosy undertones in Carrie's skin, and the orangey cast of self-tanner comes across as an athletic flush. Her hair even appears richer and a touch more golden next to the icy pink.

Bubble-icious!

☾ Pow!

56

Pale

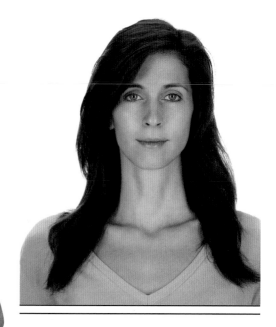

Jovanka is the rare brunette with pale blue eyes. But this pale lilac top mimics the skin tone under Jovanka's eyes, so it lends her entire face an unhealthy cast instead of bringing her unusual look into the spotlight.

◀ Fuchsia brings out the rosiness in her skin tone and makes her look healthy. Her hair color looks rich and dark, and her eyes pop.

Tomato red does nothing to emphasize Ashley's radiant complexion. Her hair looks dull set against this top, and her skin looks ruddy and blotchy.

➡ But royal blue brings Ashley's eyes and skin to life. Notice how the brassy tone her hair takes on in the first photo vanishes in the second—no touch-ups, we promise!

EARTH

Your palette is inspired by the Earth's richness—the deep greens of the forest and the warm browns of rolling hills.

Your eyes
are on the dark side: brown, green, or hazel, highlighted with orange and gold.

Your skin
is coppery, with terra-cotta undertones. You probably tan easily, and you may develop freckles in the sun.

Your hair
tends toward the brassy, and ranges from dark blonde to red to mahogany to near-black with burgundy highlights.

Icons of the Earth Colortype
include Oprah Winfrey, Susan Sarandon, Diane Lane, Rachel Bilson, Rosario Dawson, and Julianne Moore.

Your best colors:
Chocolate brown, deep teal

Your worst colors:
Cool fuchsia, pale violet

Base color:
Warm peach

60

This mauve top is too close to Eleanor's skin tone. Her cheekbones lose their luminescence, and her hair seems matte.

◀ See how much a subtle tweak can do? This deep aubergine draws out the gorgeous contrast between Eleanor's hair and skin. The flush of her cheeks comes through and her cheekbones are luminescent.

Ginger…Snap!

Angela is an iconic redhead with her warm, pale skin, and her rich hair color—a dramatic combination. Yet, somehow, this bright peony pink makes her look mousy. Its cool brightness is entirely at odds with her warm brick hair color. Even though her hair color is natural, it looks forced next to this top.

➡ Next to deep cinnabar, though, her hair seems to deepen a few shades, and her skin looks invigorated instead of anemic. This is also one of the few instances when a woman can match her lipstick to her top without looking old-fashioned!

Bad Apple

62

This acidic shade of apple green seems out of place on Marguerite, whose warm undertones come through in her hair, skin, and eyes. It's not that the shade looks bad, per se—it's just that this color makes her look immature and unsophisticated.

◄ But by darkening and deepening the shade of green, Marguerite's look goes from high school to high fashion. Earth Colortypes like Marguerite can enrich the harshness of black, white, and gray shades by wearing them with pretty forest tones like the right teal.

Pale blue—a color that many people think flatters all—makes Lisa Marie look tired. Her hair appears a little brassy, and her eyes recede into their sockets. Since Lisa Marie is not a natural blonde, she has the slightly deeper skin tone of a brunette, and the colors she wears need to balance that out.

➡ See how a more saturated shade of teal brings out her eyes and makes the brassiness in her hair color disappear? It also provides a complementary backdrop to the natural peachy glow of her cheeks and lips, making her look youthful.

STAR

Your palette is inspired by faraway supernovas bursting out of the night, from the contrast between bright lights and black sky.

Your eyes
are either pale and icy (light blue flecked with white), or super dark. Your irises may have a black line around them, separating the colored part of your eyes from the whites. If your eyes are very dark, they may be flecked with white.

Your skin
is luminescent, with a porcelain cast or olive undertones.

Your hair
is either very dark or very light—from black to platinum, dark brown to prematurely silver.

Icons of the Star Colortype
include Elizabeth Taylor, Catherine Zeta-Jones, Isabella Rossellini, and Grace Jones.

Your best colors:
Black, white, ice blue, true red

Your worst colors:
Dusty rose, terra-cotta orange

Base color:
Midnight blue

Lit Up

Jennifer's blue eyes offer an unusual contrast to her dark hair and fair, olive skin, which mid-tone colors like burnt orange do little to play up. Orange can make a natural flush appear as ruddiness, making the skin look blotchy.

← In this look, dark slate blue provides a backdrop to show off the icy blueness of Jennifer's eyes. The red lipstick lends a gorgeous pop of contrast. And the false blotchiness of her skin disappears.

In this khaki-beige turtleneck, Eliana looks like a sad 1970s schoolteacher. She is a classic example of someone who mistook her undertones for yellow, a warm color, when they are really olive, a cool color.

➡ This bright red color leaves Eliana looking sexy and vibrant and brings her into the twenty-first century. The true coolness of her skin tone is visible against the hotness of the crimson dress.

The gorgeous contrast between Renee's skin and hair makes her an iconic Star. But this muddy forest-colored top brings out her green undertones, making her look unhealthy. Cover Renee's green top with your finger to see how it interrupts the harmony of her coloring. See how her hair, eyes, and skin all make beautiful sense together without the green weighing them down?

← This rich navy, however, downplays Renee's green undertones and accents the incredible silver highlights in her hair. It unifies all the shades in her natural coloring.

Mustard yellow doesn't look great on many, but it's especially unflattering on Sarah, whose ice-blue eyes and caramel skin are lost next to the color's acidity. Like many women of mixed ethnicity, Sarah's always been told to embrace warm earth tones, but these colors do little to enhance her otherworldly eyes.

➡ An ice-blue shift that mirrors Sarah's eyes allows them to pop, and her hair and skin take on a new richness.

Blue Skies

Joe is a moon.

Jesse is a star.

What's Next?

Now that you've learned about your Colortype, glance through your closet and see how many items you already own in colors from your palette. We bet you'll find more than you might guess. Remove any clothing from your closet that is at odds with your palette, and take a look at what's left. Do you sense a new harmony among the remaining pieces of clothing? You'll be amazed at how much more sense your wardrobe makes when you take away the rogue pieces.

Now you know your Colortype—but that's just half your color story. Next, you'll combine your Colortype with your Styletype to create a totally personalized palette. The union between your natural coloring and your fashion personality is where you'll find your perfect hues.

ONE WOMAN, FOUR COLORTYPES?

A WOMAN CAN BE DIFFERENT COLORTYPES AT DIFFERENT STAGES IN HER LIFE, DEPENDING ON HOW HER HAIR AND SKIN COLORS CHANGE. MOST WOMEN WON'T BE MORE THAN TWO, BUT HOLLYWOOD, OF COURSE, REPRESENTS EXTREMES, SO YOU'LL SEE STARLETS JUMPING FROM PALETTE TO PALETTE. TAKE JENNIFER LOPEZ, FOR EXAMPLE.

With golden highlights and burnished skin, Jennifer is a Sun. This shimmering off-white dress with gold trim fits perfectly into her palette.

Jennifer Lopez looks like a Moon goddess in moonstone. Notice the cool tones of her eye shadow and her icy earrings—she's playing down the gold in her complexion and showing her cool side.

Red highlights and warm makeup make her an iconic Earth.

With pale skin and intense eye makeup, Jennifer looks like the reincarnation of Sophia Loren—and falls into the Star Colortype.

COLORTYPE: **Sun**   STYLETYPE: **Chic**

SPRING/SUMMER SIGNATURE COLOR: **Green**

FALL/WINTER SIGNATURE COLOR: **Aubergine**

Angel Sanchez and his partner, Christopher Coleman, are two of the most talented (and best-looking) guys we know. Angel's designs are all over the red carpet—on everyone from Sandra Bullock to Beyoncé, Salma Hayek to Gayle King—and Chris' designs grace some of the chicest homes across the country.

My relation with color was a slow falling-in-love process.

I'm Latino, I like drama and impact, but somehow in the beginning of my career I was afraid to experiment with colors because I didn't want to steal the attention from the line and proportion of my designs.

I used to feel better designing in black and white—it was a safe zone for me—until I realized my designs were missing something, and I understood that colors could be the best tool to give soul and variety to my ideas. I started to push myself to use colors.

These days, in each new collection I take one or two new colors to work with and see what will happen.

It's still not easy to pick the right ones. I can't work with many colors at the same time, I'd rather get into the essence of a few and explore them carefully. When I fall in love with a new color, I want to design the whole collection in that same color.

My most vivid memory of color is rolls and rolls of colorful fabric in the corner of my mom's working room.

Angel Sanchez

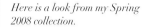

Here is a look from my Spring 2008 collection.

Here is another look from my Spring 2008 collection.

Here is my incredible partner and inspiration, Christopher Coleman.

The most colorful place in the world to me is a street of any small Caribbean town, with houses painted in different colors saturated by the light of a very strong sun.

Purple is my favorite color—it is so elegant and luxurious.

Chris helped me to understand colors and to enjoy living around them. I remember when I met him, I was moving to a new apartment. It was a minimalist white box. Then he came and painted one wall yellow and another in red, and brought in a sofa in orange—and everything changed. Now I can't live without colors around me—to me, they signify happiness and new life.

This is also a look from my Spring 2008 collection.

Fashions fade. *Style is eternal*

— Yves Saint Laurent

CHAPTER 4
DISCOVER YOUR STYLETYPE

Your Colortype takes into account your own personal coloring, but we don't expect you to feel comfortable in every color offered in your palette. That's where this chapter comes in. In this section you'll further refine which colors are best for you by determining your personal Styletype.

In our first book, *Nothing to Wear?*, we outlined the five Styletypes into which most women can be classified: Classic, Chic, Whimsical, Bohemian, and Avant-Garde. A woman's Styletype is based on her lifestyle, her style icons, her current wardrobe, and her dream image of herself. We developed the five Styletypes while working with hundreds of clients over the years.

A woman's Styletype is her fashion square one. Not only does it indicate how she looks, but also how she thinks about fashion. Does she think clothing should be decorative, or functional, or both? Does she shop to blend in, or to stand out? Does she think less is more, or more is more? Does she start, follow, or ignore trends?

Determining your Styletype is like discovering something new about yourself. When we take clients through the process of identification, they love finding out what they are. "Really? I'm an Avant-Garde? I didn't know my taste was so sophisticated!" or "I'm a Classic! I knew it!" When you identify a woman's "look," you're confirming that she has an innate sense of style tucked somewhere among the towers of sweaters on her shelves.

At first it might seem limiting to choose all of your clothing from just one (or two) Styletypes, but it's actually quite liberating. Similar to picking a flavor in an ice cream shop, making a decision between 32 flavors can be overwhelming and stressful, but choosing between 3 or 4 flavors you love will be a win-win situation.

Once you combine your Colortype and Styletype, you'll never get lost in the mall again. You'll breeze right past looks that won't flatter you and home in on ones that will. You'll be amazed to discover you actually have a well-defined sense of style, and other people will notice, too.

We won't keep you in suspense any longer—let's discover your Styletype!

Quiz: What's Your Styletype?

As you take this quiz, know that there are no right or wrong answers. Circle your first impressions—what you know about your true style is deep down in your gut. Don't intellectualize or you'll just confuse yourself.

Be sure to answer every question so your scoring will be accurate.

1. If we opened your closet, which color palette would we see?
A. Black and neutrals
B. Basics, such as navy, white, khaki, charcoal, or brown
C. Earth tones
D. A rainbow of colors
E. Black with touches of bold color

2. How would your friends describe you?
A. Playful and spirited
B. Relaxed and liberal
C. Sharp and direct
D. Traditional and proper
E. Innovative and forward-thinking

3. Given a choice, which would you rather do?
A. Throw on a pair of jeans, a T-shirt, and funky accessories
B. Step out in a fun floral dress or a bright mix of prints
C. Put on a sleek V-neck top and a modern-cut pant
D. Grab your favorite jacket, with interesting and unusual details, to wear with a black pant
E. Get comfortable in khakis, a collared shirt, and ballet flats

4. If someone gave you $200 for clothes, how would you spend it?

A. Buying a cashmere wrap
B. Purchasing a couple outfits at J.Crew or Banana Republic
C. Adding a slouchy suede bag to your accessories collection
D. Buying a dress that you're sure no one else will have
E. Splurging on anything that catches your eye

5. When you walk into a crowded room, what would you prefer to do?

A. Stand out
B. Blend in
C. Be in control; exude power
D. Seem natural and easygoing
E. Be zany and animated

6. When you have the urge (or need) to go shopping, which of the following are you most likely to do?

A. Purchase practical basics for all seasons
B. Head to the flea market for some great "lived-in" and funky finds
C. Get something with a splash of color to brighten your day
D. Find an unusual piece like nothing else in your wardrobe
E. Buy high-quality, well-tailored pieces that will always be in style

7. When you flip through the pages of fashion magazines, what is most likely to catch your eye?

A. The little black dresses worn by glam women in the party pictures
B. An editorial spread showcasing denim mixed with Moroccan textiles
C. A feature on a vintage fashion collection discovered in Austin, Texas
D. A report on new designers from Tokyo and Belgium
E. A Ralph Lauren lifestyle ad

8. Which of the following best describes the decor of your home?

A. Minimalist, architectural, and sculptural (think Jetsons)
B. Comfortable and traditional (think Cleavers)
C. Fun, kitschy, and unorthodox (think *Alice in Wonderland*)
D. Lots of rugs, earth tones, and floral prints (think '70s)
E. Streamlined, tonal, with clean surfaces (think Tom Ford)

ANSWER KEY

How'd you do? Tally the number of times your response reflected Classic, Chic, Whimsical, Bohemian, or Avant-Garde in the space provided. The high score represents your dominant style identity, your true fashion personality; the second highest score could indicate your combination style.

1: A. Chic, B. Classic, C. Bohemian, D. Whimsical, E. Avant-Garde

2: A. Whimsical, B. Bohemian, C. Chic, D. Classic, E. Avant-Garde

3: A. Bohemian, B. Whimsical, C. Chic, D. Avant-Garde, E Classic

4: A. Chic, B. Classic, C. Bohemian, D. Avant-Garde, E. Whimsical

5: A. Avant-Garde, B. Classic, C. Chic, D. Bohemian, E. Whimsical

6: A. Classic, B. Bohemian, C. Whimsical, D. Avant-Garde, E. Chic

7: A. Chic, B. Bohemian, C. Whimsical, D. Avant-Garde, E. Classic

8: A. Avant-Garde, B. Classic, C. Whimsical, D. Bohemian, E. Chic

Total Classic: _____

Total Chic: _____

Total Whimsical: _____

Total Bohemian: _____

Total Avant-Garde: _____

Your Style at a Glance

CLASSIC
Babe Paley: Simple, clean, traditional, and timeless: The colors and silhouettes in the Classic wardrobe rarely change. The Classic woman projects a ladylike image in tailored pieces made from high-quality fabrics.

CHIC
Jackie Kennedy Onassis: Chic women go for sharp lines and bold accessories. They love monochromatic, body-conscious looks and are known for their sensual approach to fashion. Some might describe them as having a European sensibility.

BOHEMIAN
Margherita Missoni: An evolution of the "rich hippie" look of the 1960s and '70s, the Bohemian Styletype combines comfort and luxury. Ethnic-inspired silhouettes, natural fabrics, and earth tones mixed with denim, leather, and suede create a messy-glam vibe.

AVANT-GARDE
Tilda Swinton: Avant-Garde women see fashion as art—they want their clothing to make a creative statement and to spark conversation. They approach shopping as collectors and take great pride in the most unusual pieces in their wardrobes.

WHIMSICAL
Sofia Coppola: The Whimsical style is playful and eclectic, but not at all messy: It's a thoughtful combination of colors and patterns. The creative possibilities and unusual colors of vintage clothing excite the Whimsical woman.

DECISIONS, DECISIONS

DOES YOUR SCORE REVEAL NO "TRUE" STYLETYPE? INSTEAD OF A BUNCH OF ANSWERS IN ONE CATEGORY, DO YOU FIND THAT YOU'RE ALL OVER THE PLACE? DON'T WORRY. OUR GUESS IS ONE OF TWO THINGS: YOU'RE A FASHION PERSON, OR YOU'VE OPTED OUT.

You're a fashion person if...
➡ You're fearless when it comes to skirt lengths and pant widths.
➡ You can name all the designers in *Vogue* and *Bazaar*.
➡ You value art over function.
➡ You think a month's paycheck is a reasonable amount to spend on a bag.

Our advice: Treat the Styletypes like a buffet. Pick and choose what you like from each category: a pair of flat suede boots from the Bohemians, a Burberry trench from the Classics, some purple tights from the Whimsicals. But beware: You must be truly brave to pull off such an eclectic look. The Fashion Person can wear whatever she wants, but she must "own" her look, or else she risks looking a wee bit nutty. What we mean by owning a look is selecting each piece with care—putting your beautiful mess together with creativity and deliberateness.

You've opted out if...
➡ You don't want to be fenced in to any particular style (or, you can't be bothered to ensure all your clothes go together).
➡ Some days you feel like a proper lady, other days you're a total tomboy.
➡ Your number one qualification for buying something is: It's on sale.
➡ You don't want to be thought of as too concerned with your image. It's what's on the inside that counts, right?

Our advice: You don't want your true purpose and message—whatever it is—to get lost in a sea of messy clothes. Caring what you look like is not shallow, it's a sign of healthy self-esteem. The last thing we want you to do if you've opted out is beat yourself up about it. Think of this as an opportunity to show the world the real you. Return to the quiz and take it again, this time as your fantasy self—the person who looks the way you really want to look. Then, use this book to become that person.

Consider each of the following Styletype collages to make sure the Styletype you've selected reflects how you see yourself—both inside and out.

CLASSIC

Traditional *Proper* **Quiet** **Formal** *Practical* Simple *Ladylike* **Tasteful** Soft-Spoken Respectful

Katharine Hepburn in *The Philadelphia Story*

CHIC

Sharp Direct Streamlined Clean **Powerful** *Effortless* *Cool* Confident Elegant **Organized**

Audrey Hepburn in *Breakfast at Tiffany's*

WHIMSICAL

Fun Playful *Colorful* Silly Young-at-Heart **Nostalgic** Freewheeling Spontaneous Unique

Sarah Jessica Parker in *Sex and the City*

BOHEMIAN

Hippie Nostalgic Free **Earthy** Relaxed *Liberal* Funky **Open-Minded** Easygoing *Warm* Inclusive

Ali MacGraw in *Love Story*

AVANT-GARDE

Edgy Smart **Intellectual** Severe Intense Innovative **Forward-Thinking** *Extreme* *Artsy* **Risk-Taking**

Meryl Streep is a Chic/Avant –Garde in *The Devil Wears Prada*

Classic Icons: Michelle Obama, Reese Witherspoon, Lena Horne, Katharine Hepburn, Grace Kelly, Diane Sawyer, Princess Diana (earlier years), Renée Zellweger

Chic Icons: Thandie Newton, Katie Holmes, Catherine Deneuve, Audrey Hepburn, Carolina Herrera, Nicole Kidman, Jacqueline Kennedy Onassis, Padma Lakshmi, Rachel Roy

Whimsical Icons: Sofia Coppola, Kirsten Dunst, Betsey Johnson, Vanessa Paradis, Gwen Stefani, Drew Barrymore, Beyoncé

Bohemian Icons: Alicia Keys, Kate Hudson, Jade Jagger, Ali MacGraw, Sienna Miller, Kate Moss, Stevie Nicks, Joss Stone

Avant-Garde Icons: Rihanna, Björk, Cate Blanchett, Marlene Dietrich, Greta Garbo, Diane Keaton, Annie Lennox, Tilda Swinton

Does Just One Styletype Feel Too Limiting?

Don't worry! Most of us are a combination of Styletypes. We express different aspects of our style personalities at different times, and in different areas, of our lives.

Maybe you're Chic on the weekends, but Classic during the week—meaning you save fashionable touches, like a flared pant or showy cuff, for play, not work. You're a Chic Classic.

Perhaps you love the combination of Whimsical touches and clean lines—a fun print in a sleek silhouette, for example. You're a Whimsical Chic.

If you have an artistic eye but prefer to keep your style statements on the subtle side, you're likely a Chic Avant-Garde.

And those who go for luxury in easygoing, ethnic-inspired silhouettes are bringing a dash of Chic to the Bohemian Styletype.

You may be wondering: How does my Colortype affect my Styletype? Each of our color palettes may be applied to any combination of Styletypes. Your Styletype dictates the way in which you wear color, not which colors you wear.

In the next chapter we'll show you how to combine the two to create an original look that's entirely you.

COLORTYPE: **Moon**   STYLETYPE: **Classic/Chic**

SPRING/SUMMER SIGNATURE COLOR: **Baby Blue**

FALL/WINTER SIGNATURE COLOR: **Purple**

Tracy Smith is the owner of House of Lavande, a vintage costume jewelry atelier in Palm Beach that supplies starlets and socialites with one-of-a-kind baubles from all eras and continents. Her own life is as colorful as her clients'.

The showroom, by appointment only, is this little jewel box. Everything is displayed where you can touch it. We encourage people to come in and play. Big white curtains open onto the Sears and Roebucks vintage tool chests filled with jewelry. Part of shopping vintage is that it's a treasure hunt, even though I consider every one of our pieces a treasure! Everything is categorized by color rather than by design or era.

About 10 years ago, I took my first trip to Provence. I was blown away by the houses and landscape. Provence awakens the senses and the imagination—I was so struck by the color in everything. I tried to re-create Provence in my house in Palm Beach, not wanting a beach home. I imported limestone, old oak floors, and French antiques.

Purple goes with everything. Mix purple with whatever and it works!

*I dress my kids in a lot of color.
Especially my little girl — she
loves Oilily. She's got these bright
blue eyes and this crazy curly
strawberry blonde hair, and a
personality to match the hair.*

*This was at the Flagler Museum in Palm
Beach. The party was for the Historical
Society with which I am involved.
The dress is one of my favorites — Zac Posen.
And of course the layering of cut crystal
necklaces from the '20s and '30s.*

Don't chase the rainbow; *create it.*

CHAPTER 5
THE STYLETYPES AND COLOR

Each of the Colortype palettes contains a wide variety of colors to choose from, but each Styletype will make use of the colors in her palette a little differently. For example, a Whimsical woman will probably wear all of the colors on her palette at one point or another, while a Chic woman will stick mostly to neutrals, and an Avant-Garde will favor blacks and whites with vivid accents.

Here are the Styletypes arranged in order of their adventurousness toward color:

(More color to less color)
Whimsical ➡ Bohemian ➡ Classic ➡ Chic ➡ Avant-Garde

Whimsical

Whimsical women have a playful attitude toward color. Iconic Whimsical designer Marc Jacobs would think nothing of combining red, pink, fuchsia, and navy, all in one outfit, and finishing up with cobalt patent-leather shoes. The Whimsical girl is cheeky, fun-loving, and unafraid of standing out. She expresses her creativity through her wardrobe, and she puts together an outfit as though she were painting a picture. She loves bright patterns and layering contrasting colors. She's not afraid of a red handbag, or yellow patent shoes. Her fashion decisions may seem haphazard but are actually deliberate—she's out to create a truly unique look that excites everyone around her. Her sense of whimsy and impulsiveness lead her to favor the brighter colors on her Colortype palette.

This shot from the Marc by Marc Jacobs Spring 2008 collection is the embodiment of the Whimsical woman's take on color. The royal blue vest and red top make one another appear more vivid, the olive shorts keep the look grounded, and the red accessories are pure fun.

Trendsetter Sofia Coppola shows off a Whimsical take on animal print in Paris.

WHIMSICAL TIPS

Choose most of the elements of your look from one color family, then "pop" the look with one unrelated color. For example, if you're wearing a blue dress, try accenting with a blue bag and red shoes.

If you're wearing a print, match accessories to one color of the print. A yellow flower or pink polka dot can inspire a genius handbag choice.

To bring spice to a monochromatic dress, try colored tights.

Bohemian

Bohemians are travelers, picking up inspiration wherever they go. This translates to rich textiles, big, ethnic jewelry, and different cultural influences combining to create a lush, multihued look. The Bohemian Styletype usually favors earth tones, deep vegetable colors, and textured fabrics such as wool, linen, and flax. Think of all the richness in a Missoni textile: tonal variations on one hue, spiked with flaxen threads for luxury. The Bohemian woman wants her clothing to serve as a map of where she's been—she dresses to tell the stories of her travels through life. She loves interesting fabrics that incorporate color naturally: paisleys, tie-dyes, ombrés, and space-dyed knits. There's noticeably less black in her wardrobe—she replaces it with denim—and there is lots of well-patined brown leather and cognac suede. Her look has the golden cast of a photograph from the 1970s, as though everything were touched by the sun.

This look from Gucci's Fall 2008 collection conveys the essence of the Bohemian vibe: rock n' roll shapes, luxurious fabrics, and exotic accessories—all thrown together with a glamorous sense of haphazardness.

Margherita Missoni, heiress to the Italian fashion empire, represents her family's luxe Bohemian style.

BOHEMIAN TIPS

Don't be afraid to mix ethnic motifs: Native American turquoise jewelry with Moroccan textiles, for example.

Go luxe with metallics. Adding gold, silver, pewter, or copper to neutrals instantly makes an outfit feel rich and decadent.

Instead of going for a cardigan or shawl, choose a hip blazer in your best neutral.

Classic

The Classic woman changes her attitude toward color according to season. In spring and summer, she favors sunny pastels and bright colors, worn with neutrals and whites. When the cooler seasons come, she builds her outfits on black, gray, and deep chocolate brown, with pops of color. She's often seen in a well-tailored navy blazer and an iconic pair of Levi's. She has a drawer of soft T-shirts in pop colors that flatter her. At night, she wears black or red. On vacation, she might step outside her comfort zone, wearing a shift dress and a pair of sexy slides in a tropical color. Across seasons, she uses scarves and bright white shirts to bring light to her face. She flatters her skin with pearl and diamond jewelry.

This 3.1 Phillip Lim look from Spring 2008 embodies the easy elegance of the Classic Styletype. Worn with white, khaki becomes a color unto itself. The starched whiteness of this easy shift dress brings out the golden tones in the model's skin, and the dark bag and warm shoes lend the look an urbane sophistication.

Babe Paley thought nothing of wearing orange pants all summer.

CLASSIC TIPS

Play with luxurious and contrasting textures. A four-ply cashmere sweater and gabardine pants in identical shades of gray will play beautifully off one another because of the way their different surfaces catch the light.

Incorporate iconic uses of color into your wardrobe: a red evening dress (think Julia Roberts in *Pretty Woman*), a yellow slicker (think Paddington Bear—and every other stylish Londoner), or a blue peacoat (thank you, navy!). A color is much less intimidating—and less likely to shock—when it has a fashion history.

Buy a fun handbag—forest green, red, even orange can look amazing with all your neutrals—but pick one in a high-quality leather or canvas so it will work well with the rest of your pieces.

Chic

The Chic woman wears all the no-color colors. She loves a monochromatic look accented with an incredible accessory: white jeans and tank top with a killer coral cuff or a gray flannel suit with an unexpected cocktail ring. She creates interest by adding texture to tonal outfits: a dramatic crocodile belt with a black sweater dress, a luxurious cashmere wrap in oatmeal worn with khakis. When she does wear higher-pigment colors, the Chic woman chooses them for subtlety: plums, burgundies, berries, and blues. Her sensibility is more European than American—wearing color in unexpected places, such as carrying a deep teal handbag instead of a black one.

For a truly modern take on Chic dressing, mix elements of scuba, origami and menswear. If only it were so simple! But Nicolas Ghesquiere, for Balenciaga, makes it seem that way, executing a variety of disparate design elements in a variety of rich, gray textures. The result? A sharp, minimalistic look that makes a major impact. Confident, edgy, and sexy, this look is for the Chic woman who sees fashion as art.

ook from the Yves Saint Laurent Fall 2008 collection is a study in tex-
Here, the lighter shades of the tweed coat and wool pants play off the
urtleneck and boots. The nubbiness of the tweed shows off the pants'
sheen, and the shine of the boots adds another visual dimension—and
h of rock and roll edge. While the signature of this chic brown look is
hness, the bittersweet chocolate lipstick is best left on the runway.

CHIC TIPS

Invest in a knockout piece of colored-stone jewelry to pair with your favorite monochromatic
looks.

Try other darks besides black: Distressed brown
riding boots look amazing with leggings; a gray
cashmere coat looks great with every winter
color, from snow white to bright red to deep
midnight blue.

Add interest to a quiet pair of wide-legged pants
with red high heels. Every time you see your toe
peek out from under that conservative hem,
you'll get a little thrill.

Avant-Garde

The Avant-Garde woman never looks boring in black. She creates interest in her wardrobe by using shape and proportion. Because she buys more "pieces" than outfits, though, she can easily incorporate the occasional pop of color into her looks. Avant-Garde women aren't afraid to really go for it when choosing pieces that will pop—they don't shy away from Day-Glo pink or mustard if it enhances the look of a piece they love. Because black can begin to look too severe after a certain age, the Avant-Garde woman must be willing to brighten her look a bit as she ages—perhaps with a cashmere sweater or a bold pair of eyeglasses.

Tilda Swinton, a true Avant-Garde, brings as much drama to her wardrobe as she does to her work. Her one-shoulder Oscar dress was a major fashion risk that paid off, projecting her confidence and intelligence.

ÜberAvant-Garde Cate Blanchett shines in this architectural black dress accented with a pop of deep fuchsia around the face.

AVANT-GARDE TIPS

Limit yourself to one accent color per outfit, so there will be a focal point to your look.

Experiment with acidic and Day-Glo shades in tiny doses—a tank, a Lucite bangle. These pieces can give even the most basic leggings-and-flats look an edge.

Though you're probably best friends with black, don't be afraid to try interesting pieces in other neutrals, like dove gray, dark olive green, or even metallics.

THE TECHNICOLOR WORLD OF MRS. KENNEDY

CHIC STAR JACKIE O. WAS AN INSPIRATION TO US IN SO MANY WAYS, ONE OF WHICH WAS HER GENIUS MASTERY OF THE ART OF MONOCHROMATIC DRESSING. SHE PROVED THAT WEARING ALL ONE COLOR IS ANYTHING BUT BORING.

Tone Trivia: *In Brazil,* gems signal the wearer's profession. Engineers wear sapphires, attorneys wear rubies, doctors wear emeralds, dentists wear topazes, professors wear green tourmalines, and merchants wear pink tourmalines.

Combining Your Styletype and Colortype

The best thing about our Colortype system is that it doesn't limit women based on their natural coloring or taste. We believe there is a shade of most every color that will work for most every woman—it's just a matter of finding it.

In the pages that follow, you'll see a series of models wearing colors from their Colortype palette in a variety of Styletypes. It's amazing to see how the models' looks actually seem to change as they morph from Classic to Chic to Avant-Garde to Whimsical to Bohemian. You'll see how different the palettes appear when expressed through different fashion attitudes.

With color one obtains an energy that seems to stem from witchcraft. —Henri Matisse, *artist*

How to Wear the Colors from Your Palette

In order to help you translate your palette to your Styletype, we've coded each shade with the Styletypes to which it's suited. The shades are organized in order from wearable-by-most to wearable-by-fewest.

Sun

Classic

Chic

Whimsical

Bohemian

Avant-Garde

Moon

Classic

Chic

Whimsical

Bohemian

Avant-Garde

Earth

Classic

Chic

Whimsical

Bohemian

Avant-Garde

Star

Classic

Chic

Whimsical

Bohemian

Avant-Garde

Crossover Colors

Here you'll see a selection of colors that cross over color types and look good on almost everyone. Fashion designers tend to include these colors in their palette because they are safe bets for women of all Colortypes.

Coral	Red	Magenta	Purple	Emerald
Turquoise	Cobalt	Midnight	Teak	Black

SUN

Sun Bohemian

A swatch of this Missoni dress could serve as a mini Sun palette. The gorgeous knit fabric incorporates peaches, yellows, greens, and khakis and is the perfect choice for a woman whose style is relaxed but not casual. If you love a multicolor look but are afraid to wear a bright print, space-dyed knits, like the ones made iconic by Missoni, are a great solution because they are tonal and easy to wear but still create a splash.

Sun Whimsical

This ensemble is a great example of a pulled-together look. The dusty rose shade that runs through both the J. Mendel jacket and the Marc Jacobs skirt ties the two pieces together, even though they are made of completely different fabrics. And see here that Whimsical doesn't necessarily mean eccentric—this outfit is totally sophisticated. The Whimsical woman just thinks outside the box when it comes to pairing pieces. All of the pieces in this ensemble could be worn by other Styletypes, just differently. For example, a Chic might wear the jacket with a pair of dark jeans, while a Bohemian could pair the skirt with a simple cashmere tank top and a pair of bejeweled sandals.

Sun Chic

Showcasing the beauty of an unconventional color is the hallmark of the Chic Styletype. Another Chic distinction is choosing a color that makes a statement, and then wearing it head to toe. The lady in emerald green, Alexander McQueen, is bound to get lots of attention.

Sun Avant-Garde

Okay, so maybe in real life you'd wear the collar down. But notice the rich shine of this incredible aubergine-satin Lanvin dress and how it seems to lend the same shine to the model's skin. Even though many Avant-Gardes build their edgy wardrobes atop a foundation of black, this dress proves that even a classic color and fabric, when executed in an interesting silhouette, can make a serious design statement.

Sun Classic

This homage to Lady Di demonstrates how a Sun can wear Classic neutrals, with a shot of peachy rose to flatter her sporty flushed cheeks. Notice how nearly every element of this look could be worn by any of the Colortypes—it's the pop of scarf that flatters Merritt's skin and leaves a strong impression.

Sun Bohemian

In another take on this Color- and Styletype combo, a coral Michael Kors dress with bead-work at the waist creates a dramatic daytime look. A great way to take an ethnic-inspired look and make it sophisticated enough for nighttime is to wear accessories in the same color.

Sun Chic

Darker-skinned Suns are born to wear metallics, like in this J. Mendel gown, especially when paired with shimmering eye makeup. If your skin is honey-colored or deeper, keep metallics a few shades lighter. If your skin is pale, choose metallics that are a few shades darker. Contrast between skin and your chosen metallic fabric is crucial to keep you from looking washed-out.

MOON

Classic Moon

A little color near the face—in the form of a vibrant patterned scarf—can do wonders for a neutral trench coat. Moon women can wear timeless khaki shades without looking washed-out, as long as they pop their complexions with bright accessories and feminine make-up, like the peachy blush and lipstick shown here.

Bohemian Moon

Combining all the no-color colors on your palette can turn a casual look into something worldly and sophisticated, even when every single piece comes from the mall. Look at the way the two shades of brown leather here play off the gray cashmere sweater, set against a backdrop of neutral denim. This is such a simple ensemble—a sweater from the Gap, vintage Levi's, and cowboy boots—but it's fashionable because of how it is styled. If you have a tiny waist, like Ashley, try layering a wide belt over your cardigan to give the look a funky edge. If you prefer not to emphasize your midsection, you can achieve a similar cool factor by layering a few long necklaces on top of one another.

Whimsical Moon

Combining pinks, yellows, and grays from the Moon palette is a hallmark of Marc Jacobs's Whimsical style—there's a lot going on, but somehow it all works. This outfit again proves that the key to keeping Whimsical witty, and not crazy, is to pull the outfit's elements from the same few colors and incorporate a basic foundation—in this case, the black tights.

Chic Moon

Chics are all about reinterpreting convention. For example, this dress is bright and the necklace is black, when things are usually the other way around! A collar-style necklace like this one is a great way to perk up the neckline of any dress. Truly adventurous Chics could try a baroque collar over a T-shirt or under a jacket for a little glamour surprise.

Avant-Garde Moon

To make an artistic statement, choose one of the less conventional colors on your palette to wear in the evening, like the emerald green of this Derek Lam top. A garment's color can contribute as much to its specialness as its cut or fabric. Take the green here: It's sort of an outlier on the Moon palette, and it's a nice break from all the blues, grays, and pinks that dominate the Moon's wardrobe. Stretch out of your comfort zone: You Avant-Gardes claim to be risk-takers, but then you spend your life in black! The unusualness of this top's color makes it feel like a piece of art—perfect for a major event.

EARTH

Bohemian Earth

The Earth palette is so well suited to the Bohemian Style-type because the warm oranges, deep greens, and saffron yellows that dominate this colorway abound on Bohemian-style clothing. Notice the warm aubergine color of the sweater: It lends a nice playfulness to a look that could otherwise appear heavy. Notice how the deep teal velvet plays up her eyes.

Classic Earth

It doesn't get more iconic than a gorgeous woman in a trench coat on a fall day. Notice that this trench is a few shades darker than the traditional khaki—it's mocha, really—so it provides enough contrast against Suzanne's warm skin tone.

116 Chic Earth

This is another take on a monochromatic evening look, this time in a deep shade of purple that flatters blonde Earths like Lisa Marie.

Whimsical Earth

The metallic print on this dress from H&M is surprisingly subtle and reflects warm light toward the face: The dress would be perfect for a candlelit dinner.

Some Earth women might dismiss metallics for fear they are too flashy, but this look proves the subtlety of the right ones. See how the pewter background of the dress is much deeper than the model's skin tone? The darker the metallic, the less reflective it is. The shades of peach, orange, and yellow in the print play off the model's skin and hair.

118

Avant-Garde Earth

The way the burgundy velvet of this Gaultier dress catches the light provides a gorgeous echo of the model's warm hair. Isn't it incredible how porcelain her skin appears when she wears such a dark color? Since Earth girls wear so many mid-tone colors in their daily lives, a superdark dress provides a glorious element of glamour and surprise. And the dramatic dropped back and tulip skirt of this style turn classic materials like silk and velvet into an Avant-Garde piece.

Chic Earth

Could there be a more gorgeous dress for an elegant party on a cold night? This burgundy-rose color reflects the highlights in Suzanne's hair and makes her eyes pop. Even though this dress offers a lot of coverage—all that's showing is Suzanne's sinewy arms—the way its sheen highlights all the right places makes it subtly sexy. And that's chic.

STAR

☆

Whimsical Star

This Zac Posen dress combines two of Star's best colors in a fresh, swingy silhouette. The red and magenta here step tonal dressing up a notch (remember analogous colors?), and the loose silhouette gives the dress a relaxed, casual feeling. This would be a great dinner look on a warm vacation, or the perfect look for a day of shopping and a fancy lunch with the girls.

Bohemian Star

Ethnic-inspired prints work beautifully on those with high-contrast coloring. Notice the black base and bright details of this vintage Etro. The key to keeping Bohemian looks from becoming sloppy is to combine ethnic-inspired fabrics with classic silhouettes, and vice versa. For example, if this dress were to appear in a solid color, it could be interpreted as very Chic, even Classic. And the pattern, if executed in a simple shift dress, could also be worn by Chic or Classic Styletypes.

Classic Star

Whether you're into fake fur or the real thing—what's this one, you ask? not telling!—a soft, tactile white jacket recalls glamorous 1950s movies in which women wore high-heeled slippers and slept in their makeup. We're not suggesting you do either of those things—well, the slippers, maybe. But notice how the luxurious winter white of this pullover contrasts with Cindy's shiny black hair. Worn with an evening gown or a great pair of jeans, this soft piece brings drama and luxury to the Classic Star's wardrobe.

Classic Star

Talk about Hollywood glamour! Sure, this Angel Sanchez dress would steal the spotlight at any awards show, but that doesn't mean you can't wear it to a nighttime wedding, or even a Christmas party. If you think the tail seems too dramatic, focus on the gorgeous (and flattering!) bodice and how dynamite this red looks next to Cindy's hair and skin.

Chic Star

In this indigo Alaïa gown, Jennifer looks sophisticated and sexy. In true Chic style, we've added a necklace in a similar hue to make a mono-chromatic statement. Never underestimate the power of a chunky necklace near your face to create maximum drama with minimum effort.

Avant-Garde Star

There's no question, this one is a showstopper. And yes, it's black! Some of you may be thinking, "Finally." Of course, we're not telling you to donate all your black clothing to Goodwill—we understand that black has been the foundation color for fashionable women since Victorian times. We just want you to see how many more choices you have beyond black, so that when you return to black, it seems special and dramatic, rather than automatic. This Yohji Yamamoto piece is so flattering because of its open neck. The deep, broad neckline reveals Jennifer's luminous skin, drawing attention to her cleavage and bone structure, and keeps the world's darkest color from looking heavy or stifling.

COLORTYPE: **Star**	STYLETYPE: **Classic/Chic/Avante-Garde**
SPRING/SUMMER SIGNATURE COLOR: Moss Green	
FALL/WINTER SIGNATURE COLOR: Eggplant	

We met Amy through mutual friends in the fashion world. She is a brilliant writer (she's the author of *The God of Driving,* among other things) and a correspondent for *Vanity Fair* magazine, for which she presides over the International Best-Dressed List. Of course, she also has a brilliant sense of her own style.

Color is a mood shifter, a reflection or enhancement of an interior state, and a way to modify the state of mind or delight the eyes of others. Color is to the eye what music is to the ears and love to the heart.

I like going from wearing neutrals—grays, blacks, navy—to the optical shock of poison green or burnt orange, and then back to neutrals again. I love all colors, and all color combinations—but in my clothing and decor I gravitate to a palette of purples, aubergines, plums, violets, lilacs, and pinks.

The most colorful place I've ever been is my own home. I use color fearlessly. I don't believe any colors clash. Flowers, fish, birds, and sunsets have suggested to me that all colors can harmonize beautifully.

Style is most potent when
it is *least complicated.*

— Tom Ford

CHAPTER 6
WEARING
YOUR
COLORS

W e mentioned earlier that we don't want to encourage people to walk around in head-to-toe pink pantsuits. We should also mention that we're against: orange jumpsuits, red tracksuits, and nude bodysuits, unless you're wearing them under your clothing. (And we're not really fans of matching your lipstick and your nails to your blouse, but we'll get to makeup later.)

An easy way to avoid looking dated, no matter your Styletype, is to use black, white, neutrals, and colors that pop. What we mean when we employ this sweet metaphor is that neutrals will make up the bulk of your wardrobe, and pop colors will provide accents and personality.

Obviously, the most neutral of the neutrals is black. It looks good on everyone. It makes us look skinny and put-together. It makes our skin shine, even when we're tired. It's true that, worn incorrectly, black can seem a little…sad. That's why we'd never relegate you to an all-black look, especially when you're feeling down or low-energy. But black, when accented with pop shades from your palette, can be the foundation for any look, from casual daytime to nighttime drama.

THE BEST BLACK

WHEN GIVEN OPTIONS BETWEEN DIFFERENT BLACKS, ALWAYS CHOOSE THE DARKEST ONE. NEVER WEAR AN OUTFIT COMPOSED OF A MIX OF VARYING SHADES OF BLACK.

This can look cheap and messy. If a black garment you love is faded, pair it with colors other than black so the fading is less obvious, or try it with highly textured black pieces, such as a tailored velvet jacket or a nubby cashmere sweater.

The Basics

By investing in these simple black or dark neutral items, you'll create a capsule wardrobe and you'll have everything you need to make up the cake of your wardrobe. If you prefer dark neutrals such as brown, charcoal, or navy, you can certainly purchase your cake in those colors. More on this later.

CLOTHING

Flattering pants, a fitted jacket, and a knee-length pencil skirt, all in the same fabric (Gabardine, wool, or twill—all with a bit of stretch—are our favorites.)

Be sure to go with classic styling on these pieces, so they won't seem dated after a season or two. Avoid lots of pockets, severely belled or tapered legs, and fabrics with too much shine.

A little dress, or two—ideally, one for day and one for night (If you can only afford one, choose a knee-length style with an open neckline, which you can dress up or down.)

A great pair of flattering dark denim jeans

A pair of matte black leggings (Full-length, please—save the pedal pushers for spin class.)

A tank top, a V-neck T-shirt, and a turtleneck in a high-quality cotton knit fabric (Hand-wash these if you want them to hold their color.)

Three pairs of matte, opaque tights (If you have money to spend, try Wolford; if you're on a budget, Club Monaco's are high-quality. Make sure they are very, very dark, and not at all shiny, unless you are auditioning for a workout video.)

A tailored jacket that can be worn both indoors and outdoors (Leather, cotton canvas, corduroy, cashmere, and suede are our favorite materials.)

Mix and match all these pieces as the foundation for your wardrobe.

A CAPSULE-WARDROBE RESOURCE GUIDE FOR EVERY STYLETYPE

YOU MIGHT BE WONDERING, SHOULDN'T THE CAPSULE-WARDROBE ITEMS DIFFER FROM STYLE-TYPE TO STYLETYPE? NO. WHAT WILL DIFFER WILL BE THE WAY THE PIECES ARE INTERPRETED THROUGH DESIGN, CUT, FIT, AND FABRIC.

Take, for example, the "quintessential" black pant: For a Classic woman, it's slim and well-tailored, with a high-ish waist. For a Chic, the rise is a little lower and the leg opening a little looser. A Whimsical might want a much wider leg and pockets on the backside. Maybe a Bohemian's ideal pant has a touch of flare. And for an Avant-Garde, subtle zippers on the ankles or tuxedo stripes along the sides add that extra element that defines her style.

To find capsule pieces you love, just shop stores and designers that suit your style. Here's an easy guide.

Classic:
Agnona, Akris, Anne Klein, Ann Taylor, Brooks Brothers, Burberry, Eileen Fisher, Gap, J.Crew, Lacoste, Lilly Pulitzer, Liz Claiborne, Loro Piana, Michael Kors, Ralph Lauren, Talbots, Theory

Chic:
Armani, Banana Republic, Benetton, Calvin Klein, Chanel, Club Monaco, DKNY, Donna Karan, Express, Gucci, H&M, INC, Kenneth Cole, Lanvin, Laundry, The Limited, Max Mara, Narciso Rodriguez, Valentino, Zara

Whimsical:
Betsey Johnson, Chloe, Forever 21, French Connection, Louis Vuitton, Marc by Marc Jacobs, Marc Jacobs, Milly, Nanette Lepore, 3.1 Phillip Lim, Prada, Vera Wang

Bohemian:
Anthropologie, Dolce & Gabbana, Elie Tahari, Etro, H&M, Matthew Williamson, Missoni, Roberto Cavalli, Urban Outfitters

Avant-Garde:
Alexander McQueen, Balenciaga, Comme des Garçons, Jean-Paul Gaultier, John Galliano, Lanvin, Proenza Schouler, Topshop, Viktor & Rolf, Yohji Yamamoto, Yves Saint Laurent

ACCESSORIES

A large tote in high-quality leather, nylon, or canvas (When choosing leather, go for texture: pebble-grained or mock-croc will withstand everyday wear and add richness to your look.)

Women are always asking us whether status bags—which, these days, cost more than some small cars—are worth it. We think the look of a bag, not its price, is most important, so don't go into debt when you can find amazing choices at stores such as Zara, Banana Republic, and H&M. That said, quality in leather goods really varies, so buy the best craftsmanship you can afford. Look for bags with full linings and stitches that look well-finished and tight. Finally, the number one element that makes a handbag last: those four little metal feet on the bottom of well-made totes. They'll keep the bottom of your bag from touching the ground, thus keeping it free from dirt, and the surface of the leather safe from scratching.

A pair of flat, knee-high boots in high-quality leather (If you can't afford high-quality leather, go for suede—it just looks more expensive, even when it's not.)

A pair of the best pumps you can afford (Manolo Blahnik, Christian Louboutin, and Prada are phenomenal if you want to drop some serious cash; Nine West, Zara, and H&M make shockingly affordable ones.)

A selection of black jewelry—price is unimportant, just choose what you love—including jet (or imitation-jet) necklaces, Bakelite bangles, chunky collars, and a velvet ribbon on which to string your favorite vintage brooches and pendants.

Everybody Needs a Pop

You've probably heard someone creative in your life—a decorator, an artist, a florist—refer to the importance of a focal point, a clear area on which the eye can focus, when discussing a room, painting, or floral arrangement. Outfits need focal points, too—and the easiest way to create them is with color.

Maybe you're afraid to buy bright clothes or accessories because of the attention they will draw to you. But life is all about risks. Four-star chefs earn their status because they develop a flavor signature. One strong flavor can bring new complexity to subtler ones, and the same is true for adding pops of color to your wardrobe. The best way to breathe new life into your favorite black dress, white shirt, khaki jacket, or olive green sweater is to put them next to an unexpected jolt of brightness.

The way to create a pop is through contrast. You don't necessarily need to choose a loud color to bring depth and complexity to your look; you just need to combine colors that are significantly different from one another. This strategy is the opposite of tonal dressing, combining many shades of the same color. Instead, create interest in a neutral outfit by adding a jolt of hot-pink cashmere, or invigorate a black dress with a red beaded necklace. You can even tie a multicolor print scarf to the strap of a handbag for a bit of whimsical fun.

Just as we suggest keeping an arsenal of basic black pieces in your closet, we also recommend you purchase a capsule of items in your favorite pop colors. Mixing items from your pop-color capsule with your black pieces will inject your wardrobe with life and personality. These items are often affordable, so you may want to buy them in more than one color—a dark pop for fall and winter, a light one for spring and summer.

While black is the quintessential foundation—it gives your look a base, adds length to your body, and keeps your silhouette sleek and narrow—your look still needs a dash of you, courtesy of some pop-color frosting. Splashes of color brighten your complexion, keep black from being boring, and lend individuality to your style.

The Pop-Color Capsule

A thin cashmere or cotton sweater for layering under jackets

A heavy-gauge cashmere or wool sweater

A pashmina or another kind of cozy wrap

A tank top and a T-shirt in high-quality cotton

A pair of suede, leather, or canvas ballet flats

A fun clutch

A few pieces of jewelry—costume or fine

You might be shocked by how many looks you can get out of your neutral foundation and pop color capsules.

But black is just one foundation option. Some women prefer to purchase their capsule wardrobe in a neutral color, like chocolate, charcoal, or khaki. You can wear your neutral foundation pieces in the same way you would wear your blacks, but choosing the right neutral can be tricky. We'll help you find just the right ones for your particular coloring. More on that in a minute.

To create outfits using your capsule wardrobes, just combine any number of black pieces with one piece in a pop color. This formula is essentially foolproof. Once you've got the hang of the black-plus-pop equation, you'll be ready to layer in some neutrals.

JEWELRY IN COLOR

PERHAPS THE EASIEST — AND CERTAINLY ONE OF THE MOST EFFECTIVE — WAYS TO INCORPORATE A POP COLOR IS WITH A PIECE OF COLORFUL JEWELRY. WHETHER IT COSTS $5 OR $5,000 ISN'T THE POINT — JUST CHOOSE SOMETHING THAT EXCITES YOU. A NEUTRAL LOOK CAN GO FROM BLAH TO WOW WITH THE ADDITION OF A PAIR OF CORAL DROP EARRINGS, OR A TURQUOISE CUFF, OR AN AMETHYST COCKTAIL RING. THE CHOICE IS YOURS — JUST LOOK AT THE BRIGHTER COLORS ON YOUR PALETTE FOR INSPIRA-TION. TRACY, OWNER OF HOUSE OF LAVANDE, SHARED SOME OF HER FAVORITE PIECES WITH US.

Nothing works better with a strapless neckline than a dramatic necklace. This piece combines lots of materials without looking hodge-podge. The reason the look remains sophisticated, not overdone? The simple brown and gold palette of the rest of the outfit.

What could be more romantic than a drapey, Grecian gown paired with monochromatic jewelry? When you want a subtle, feminine look, it's fine to keep your jewelry in the same color family as your clothing—provided the color is one that flatters you!

Tracy Smith and her friend and publicist, Amy Lagae

Here are some extraordinary vintage pieces from Lavande to inspire you.

"I love to throw in color in the accessory, no matter what I'm wearing," says Tracy Smith, "I may feel like layered crystal necklaces, or an unconventional color combination, like purple and yellow—just what feels good that day." This sense of joy and freedom is the key to wearing vibrant jewelry.

Sun

Moon

Earth

EVERYONE!

Star

Isn't this the most glamorous color wheel you've ever seen?

Choosing Your Neutrals Wisely

It's easy to see why neutrals like khaki and cream, and all the gray-beige colors in between, appeal to most of us—they can be like a second skin. You don't need to worry about matching a top to a pair of khaki pants: Everything goes. A washed-canvas safari jacket is so versatile, it can be thrown on over a pair of jeans and a tank or a little black dress.

> If I see everything in gray, and in gray all the colors which I experience and which I would like to reproduce, then why should I use any other color?
> — Alberto Giacometti, *artist*

But the sneaky thing about neutrals is that they're not actually "neutral" in the truest sense of the word. Like our skin, these colors have complex undertones, which may or may not flatter our complexions. Neutrals are not one-tone-fits-all.

Take khaki. The word "khaki" comes from the Urdu language, and it means "yellow-brown dust." But in English, you often hear the term "khaki green." So, what we think of as khaki, the number one selling color of men's pants in the United States, is actually a range of colors, from dusty yellow to green to brown.

You think it doesn't matter what color your pants are? Wrong. Your pants need to make sense with the rest of your wardrobe, which, of course, will consist only of shades in your Colortype palette by the time you've finished reading this book. Your pants also need to be in sync with your skin tone. And neutrals, naturally, don't appear only on pants, but also on sweaters, T-shirts, blouses, dresses, coats, and jackets, too.

How, then, to choose the best neutral for you? (No, it's not okay to grab whichever pair of pants is on the Banana Republic sale table.) Here are our golden (or sandy, or olive, or gray!) rules:

If the fabric color is too close to your skin color, walk away. A neutral needs to be discernibly lighter or darker than you are, so you won't disappear into it. You'll want as much contrast as possible.

When in doubt, darker is better. Neutrals with higher color saturations seem more luxurious somehow. These fabrics likely have more body and better drape because they haven't been heavily abraded in a washing process meant to soften them and lighten their color. (Leave the shredded Abercrombie lowriders to the kiddies.)

This is a situation where you'll want to avoid your own undertones. (For example, if you have olive skin, you shouldn't wear an olive green sweater.) The shades of peach and red and pink and brick hiding beneath our epidermis are what make us look healthy and vibrant. And they can disappear entirely when their sallow counterpoints—greens and yellows—are emphasized. What about those women with lovely, peachy undertones? Even they can make the most of their skin by wearing neutrals in strong, contrasting shades.

Virtually every item in the black capsule wardrobe will work well in neutral colors as well, but you don't need to have everything—just choose which items you'd like. We adore military and safari jackets in various shades of beige, olive, and khaki, and cashmere and wool pants and sweaters in every shade of gray. Our least favorite neutral items are T-shirts and other cotton knits; you're better off with black, white, or a pop color, since neutrals can look muddy in this fabrication.

NOT STAYING NEUTRAL

SOMETIMES IT'S DIFFICULT TO FIND A BROAD RANGE OF PIECES IN FUN COLORS, ESPECIALLY DURING A SEASON WHEN EVERY DESIGNER SEEMS TO GO NEUTRAL. HERE ARE SOME STORES AND WEB SITES THAT WON'T DISAPPOINT YOU:

American Apparel (for T-shirts)

Neiman Marcus, Bloomingdales, Saks Fifth Avenue, Macy's (for private-label knits and sweaters, especially cashmere)

J.Crew (for knits, fun dresses, flats, and flip-flops)

French Sole (for colorful ballet flats)

Anthropologie (for fanciful sweaters, knits, and dresses)

C&C California, James Perse, Three Dots, and Sweetees (for fine-gauge cotton knits)

H&M, Toolshop (for trends)

Here's which neutrals will work best for the range of skin tones within each Colortype. Black is a no-brainer neutral. We did not include it here because almost everyone can wear it and it's much more creative to seek out other neutrals that flatter your skin.

☾ MOON

Complexion	Go For...	Stay Away From...
Fair	Cool Stone	Warm Beige
Medium	Dove Gray	Warm Khaki
Dark	Midnight Navy	Chocolate Brown

☆ STAR

Complexion	Go For...	Stay Away From...
Fair	Dove Gray	Mustard Khaki
Medium	Charcoal Gray	Warm Beige
Dark	Bright White	Olive Green

☼ SUN

Complexion	Go For...	Stay Away From...
Fair	Warm Khaki	Cool Stone
Medium	Ivory	Cool Olive
Dark	Chocolate Brown	Steel Gray

🌏 EARTH

Complexion	Go For...	Stay Away From...
Fair	Camel	Dove Gray
Medium	Brownish Khaki	Cool Stone
Dark	Light Putty	Olive Green

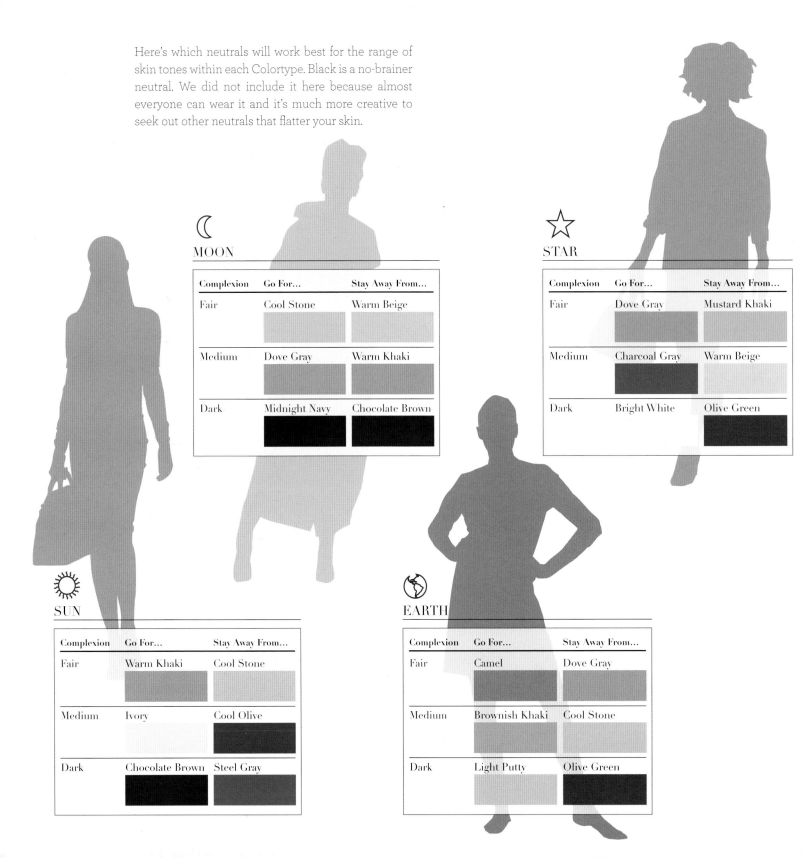

A NOTE ON DENIM

Denim is probably the most popular neutral in the world. Its comfort, durability, and goes-with-everything indigo hue make it a staple in most everyone's closet.

Although there are endless options, choosing a denim shade is easy: Dark indigo, black, and resin are most flattering. As a rule, darkest denims are best for nighttime, and lighter, more casual washes work well for day or on weekends.

Make sure your closet is stocked with these quintessential items in classic dark blue:

A pair of great-fitting jeans with straight—not belled or pegged—legs

A tailored jean jacket

A knee-length, A-line denim skirt

These pieces will work with your blacks, your neutrals, and your pops, so you'll be wearing them often!

Winning Combinations

Now that you have a strong base for your wardrobe, it's time to have a bit of fun! You can mix colors and avoid looking loony as long as you know what you're doing.

Some color combinations are like peanut butter and jelly—they just go together. (Incidentally, nut brown with deep purple is very sophisticated.)

The most successful shade pairings bring out the best in one another, whether through contrast or similarity. Colors can completely change one another's appearance.

The red squares below look like two different shades, right?

They're not. They just look different depending on whether they are adjacent to a white or a green square.

This optical illusion proves the importance of pairing colors that enhance one another. Worn with the wrong shade of green, your new fuchsia sweater might look rather tomatoey! (Not to mention the fact that everyone will be wishing you a Merry Christmas, even in February.)

Here are a few surefire ways to know that colors will look good together:

They are positioned across from one another on the color wheel. This means they are complementary colors and balance one another out.

One is a neutral, like gray or khaki, and the other is a bright or pastel. Mixing a no-color color with a more intense hue means they're unlikely to clash.

They share the same undertone. For example, a pair of heathered, deep blue–gray pants will look brilliant with a light slate blue cashmere sweater.

There are also some color combos to stay far away from, mostly because they carry a cultural meaning that will take the focus off you and remind people of goofy holidays or fast-food restaurants. These combos are:

Orange and black. Trick or treat: Need we say more?

Red and yellow. Would you like fries with that?

Yellow and black. Don't sting me, honey.

Red, white, and blue. Show your patriotism with your vote, not your wardrobe.

Red and green. Even Santa has the good sense to avoid this combination.

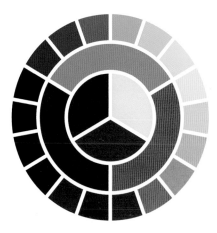

COLOR UNDERCOVER

THERE'S NO LAW AGAINST CUTE UNDERWEAR. THOUGH SOMETIMES IT FEELS LIKE WOMEN ARE FOLLOWING SOME UNSPOKEN CODE, PURCHASING BRAS AND PANTIES ONLY IN NUDE AND BLACK. WHILE THESE NEUTRAL FOUNDATION GARMENTS ARE KEY, THERE'S ALSO A WHOLE COLORFUL WORLD OF LINGERIE WAITING TO BE EXPLORED. THIS ADORABLE SET IS FROM H&M.

If you're looking for a no-brainer, check out our favorite combinations by Colortype below.

SUN

Coral and chocolate

Dove gray and lavender

Butter yellow and deep purple

MOON

Dior gray and robin's-egg blue

Gray flannel and Kelly green

Pale pink and navy

EARTH

Chocolate and navy

Olive and brown

Chocolate and raspberry

STAR

Midnight blue and black

Navy and fuchsia

White and cognac

BAD COLORS AND THE WOMEN WHO LOVE THEM

JUST AS IN RELATIONSHIPS, SOMETIMES WE LOVE SOMETHING THAT DOESN'T LOVE US BACK. MAYBE YOU'RE AN EARTH INFATUATED WITH FLUORESCENT PINK, BUT EVERY TIME YOU PUT ON THAT AMERICAN APPAREL TANK YOU JUST HAD TO HAVE, YOU LOOK SEA-SICK. PERHAPS THAT OFF-WHITE CASHMERE WRAP YOUR MOTHER-IN-LAW FOUND FOR YOU AT THE SAKS SALE SHOULD HAVE STAYED THERE. WHATEVER YOUR DILEMMA, WE HAVE TIPS ON HOW TO SALVAGE MISGUIDED CLOTHING BUYS, OR INDULGE ANEW IN COLORS THAT AREN'T ON YOUR PALETTE.

① Don't wear unflattering colors near your face.

② If you're not sure whether a color flatters your complexion, break up its impact by layering it with pieces in white or a flattering tonal color.

③ Never underestimate the power of a good mani-pedi—if you love bright orange, try it on your toes!

④ Try to find your "bad" colors incorporated into prints that also include your "good" colors.

⑤ Try layering a scarf in a flattering color over an unflattering top. This tip isn't just for preppy Hermès junkies—it also will work with a chunky wool number (à la J.Crew).

Monochromes: A Baby Step into the World of Color

Ironically, sometimes the best way to coax a black-addict over the rainbow is to encourage head-to-toe one-color dressing. We're not suggesting you try on yards and yards of emerald, but a look in various tones of chocolate brown or eggplant could have all the chic subtlety of that little black dress with a skin-brightening bonus. Plus, you'll stand out in the crowd. To keep monochrome from becoming monotone, play with texture. Since everything you're wearing will be the same color, people will notice subtle details in the way each fabric catches the light. Try pairing smooth gabardine pants with a nubby boiled-wool sweater, or a silk jersey top with rugged denim.

> For a long time I limited myself to one color—as a form of discipline. —Pablo Picasso, *artist*

Color and Aging

As we age, our vision yellows, which can result in what seems like a permanent state of melancholy and wardrobe ennui. When colors look sallow, it's hard to get excited about them and all too easy to give up on color altogether. Many women make the mistake of toning down their hair, makeup, and wardrobe in an attempt, perhaps, to go silently into that good night. We say: Stop it! Enjoy your golden age.

Marianne is a client who was crossing the threshold into retirement. Her formerly flame-red hair was beginning to gray, her green eyes seemed more tired than they used to, and the rosy cheeks people had commented on all her life had gone on strike.

Her impulse, when shopping with Jesse, was to buy "black, black, black!" She felt that wearing color drew too much attention to her when she wasn't feeling her best. "Black is what young people wear," she explained. "It's slimming!" Jesse had to remind her that she didn't have a weight problem, and skinnier doesn't always read younger.

Jesse coaxed Marianne into trying some rich berry-colored cashmere sweaters. He pulled an old pair of emerald earrings out of her jewelry archive to play off her eyes. And he sent her to the salon for her very first dye job—a rinse that restored the flame to her hair. Needless to say, she was glowing.

GOING GRAY

WE ALL KNOW ABOUT THE DULLING PROCESS THAT COMES WITH AGING, BUT WHY?

Hair goes gray because as follicles age, they produce less melanin, the pigment that gives hair its color. The age at which one's hair goes gray is usually genetically determined, and while the process can be masked beautifully with hair color, it can't be stopped with vitamins or drugs.

Skin also loses pigment-producing cells, but the ones that remain show up as age spots. It also appears duller because the body produces less oil, leaving skin flaky and dry. Moisturizer becomes necessary to give skin that ever-elusive glow.

Nails can become thick and yellowed as a result of various medical conditions that come with aging—or simply too much dark polish! To whiten them, use a paste of baking soda and hydrogen peroxide applied with a Q-tip.

Here are some tips for those who fear they're losing their luster:

If your hair is going white, take care of it. We don't mean you have to restore it to its youth, but you can't just let it languish in a state of yellow-gray. White hair is gorgeous and flattering to most skin tones, but salt-and-pepper, or more accurately, chicken-soup-and-pepper, is not. If you're not sure what to do, consult a colorist. He or she can let you know your options, from brightening dishwater gray to returning to teenage flax.

Don't be afraid of makeup. Gray eyebrows and lashes need pencil and mascara in order not to disappear. A little peachy pink blush on the apples of the cheeks will brighten the whole face. And some pale gloss will seem to restore lips to their former poutiness.

Imagine this: It's against the law to wear black. What would you wear instead? Now go out and buy something in that color, before you lose your nerve! If you're a Sun, try a rich saffron yellow to make the most of the golden tones in your skin. If you're a Moon, dove gray will perk up your complexion and bring out the light in your eyes. Those in the Earth Colortype will look gorgeous in deep plum, and Stars—especially those with silver or white hair—will sparkle in ice blue.

Don't overinvest in no-color colors like oatmeal, taupe, and ecru, even those that appear on your Colortype palette. These can appear too close to your natural skin tone and wash you out. As a general rule, the more pigment you lose from your skin and hair, the more you should add to your wardrobe.

Incorporate color into your jewelry. Their brilliance will bring you to life—even if it's just because your love for them shows in your face. Be sure to choose colored stones that fit into your Colortype palette for maximum flattery. Here are some suggestions:

SUN:
Citrine, amber, yellow tourmaline

MOON:
Aquamarine, sapphire, turquoise

EARTH:
Emerald, garnet, topaz, fire opal

STAR:
Ruby, opal, pearl

SUN

Helen Mirren looks fantastic in one of the deepest colors on her palette—jade green. Notice how it really maximizes the subtle blush on her cheeks and her flaxen hair.

MOON

Glenn Close repeats the stunning aquamarine of her eyes in her gown and her earrings. Pretty rose lipstick is a soft complement to her skin tone.

EARTH

Patti La Belle shows how flattering a range of hues in the same color family can be. Notice how the rich brown of her jacket plays off her caramel skin tone, and the highlights in her hair are reflected in the pattern on her wrap.

STAR

Model and muse Carmen Dell'Orefice is stunning with white hair. Notice how she draws attention to it with her white blouse, intense smoky eyes, and youthful rose lips.

Color and Your Shape

Color not only brings out the sparkle in your hair, skin, and eyes, but it also does some serious shape-shifting for your figure. Think of two identical cars next to one another: one black, one white. The white one looks bigger, right? That's because it reflects light, rather than absorbs it.

You've probably seen tummy-slimming bathing suits promising to turn an apple into an hourglass. Of course these wonders make use of the power of spandex, but they also use color to create a slimming effect. Notice how they often use panels of black at the sides of the waist, with a brighter color in the center. This is to create the illusion of a thin waist, by using black to mimic negative space. The suit fools the eye into thinking your width stops at the edges of the color.

We take a subtler approach to using color for shapeshifting, and we have suggestions specific to each of three body types: straight, curvy, and full.

Straight body types are lean and gamine, meaning there's not much of a difference among their bust, waist, and hip measurements. These ladies have a low body-fat percentage and might be described as lanky or athletic.

Curvy body types are icons of femininity, true hourglasses. They have classic womanly proportions: a full bust, a waist that narrows significantly, and hips that mirror the width of their shoulders.

Full body types have a little extra padding all over.

Just as you can be a combination of Styletypes and Colortypes, you can be a combination of body types.

For example, someone who's Straight/Curvy might have a large chest but narrow hips. A Full/Curvy woman has model proportions, with everything just a bit larger.

Just as you can enhance and camouflage elements of your shape with cut and fabric, you can use color to create slimming and lengthening illusions. As you already know, bright colors create expansion and darker ones make things seem smaller. Here are some more tips by body type.

STRAIGHT

To enhance a smallish bust, pair a close-fitting knit (a T-shirt in spring and summer, a sweater in fall or winter) in one of the brighter colors on your palette with your favorite pair of jeans or a darker colored skirt or pant.

To add the illusion of fullness, choose lighter neutrals over darker ones. For example, try beige bootcut cords with a light heather-gray cashmere sweater and natural off-white shearling boots.

When attending a formal event, don't be afraid to go for a dress in a pop color rather than black or a neutral. Those red, yellow, and blue frocks were made for clothes hangers like you!

CURVY

At the risk of sounding like *Saturday Night Live* versions of Gap employees ("You gotta cinch that!"), we'll say that belts are the curvy girl's best friend. They break up the line between the shoulders and the hips, calling attention to the slimmest—and most feminine—part of a woman's body. Finding your "natural" waist can be confusing when fashion trends send it seesawing up and down every season. In terms of finding the right place to put your belt, the answer is simple: Find your skinniest latitude. Sometimes it can be hard to judge your own size, so get technical: Use a tape measure to check your waist at different points, and belt at the smallest measurement. When choosing belts, go beyond the traditional black and brown and try silk obis (the gorgeous textiles traditional geisha wear over their kimonos) or wider, retro-style belts in patent leather.

Concentrate bright colors on the areas you want to emphasize, and dark colors on the areas you want to slim. This sounds like a no-brainer, but we're amazed by how many busty women we see in pink and purple clingy knits.

Try a nipped-waist, full-skirted dress in a bright, feminine print. Look at romantic photos of 1950s starlets to inspire you.

FULL

For overall slimming, choose a dark, monochromatic look. No, we are not insisting larger women cover themselves with head-to-toe black. We are suggesting that you start with a long, clean line, and use accessories and outerwear pieces to give your look interest. In addition to black, try charcoal, chocolate brown, navy, midnight blue, burgundy, and deep aubergine, or whichever other dark colors you find in your Colortype palette.

More tips for slimming:

Dark pieces should fit close to the body, while brighter ones should float over curves, skimming their surface.

On a warm-weather vacation, a combination of ethereal white separates will be more flattering than a monochromatic look in a bright color.

Match your shoe color to your pant color to create length.

Match your belt color to your pant color to streamline your middle.

What they say about stripes is true: Vertical ones make you look longer, horizontal ones make you look wider. Either way, stripes have to be subtle, otherwise you look like wallpaper. And choose stripes in nonclingy woven fabrics instead of knits—if the stripes on a too-tight garment get distorted, your shape will look as though you're in a funhouse mirror.

Try a bright, fun jacket or cardigan over a monochromatic look for a special event.

Choose tonal prints with a dark background.

PATTERN RECOGNITION

WE'VE ALL HEARD THAT BIG PATTERNS MAKE YOU LOOK BIG, AND SMALL ONES MAKE YOU LOOK SMALL. WHILE THIS MAY BE PARTIALLY TRUE, WE THINK THAT WHETHER A PRINT IS FLATTERING HAS MORE TO DO WITH ITS COLORATION THAN ITS SIZE. FOR EXAMPLE, A LARGE, TONAL FLORAL PRINT MADE UP OF DEEP BLUES AND PURPLES WILL BE MORE SLIMMING THAN A TINY FLORAL PRINT MADE UP OF A COMBINATION OF BRIGHT COLORS (LIKE PINKS, YELLOWS, AND ORANGES).

Here's how to find your prints charming:

Choose a pattern to match your Styletype. Floral prints are romantic, animal prints are sexy, and geometric prints are fashion-forward.

Where you place the pattern is as important as what it looks like. Avoid printed pants unless you're a size 2 living in Palm Beach. Avoid printed knits once you've been through puberty.

Collecting a few iconic prints is a fun way to bring whimsy and value to your wardrobe. For example, the lipstick print by Prada memorialized by Charlotte on *Sex and the City* has increased in value since its inception.

There's an ideal print for each Styletype. Classic women look great in stripes and plaids. Bohemians should go for ombre fabrics and animal prints. Chic women can incorporate tone-on-tone graphic prints into their monochromatic looks. Whimsical gals are at home in bright florals. And Avant-Gardes look cool in colorblocked styles.

Know, first, who you are; *then adorn yourself* accordingly.

— Epictetus

CHAPTER 7
COLOR AND THE MIND

Color has a powerful impact on our emotions and actions. Just seeing a certain color can change the way someone feels, as well as their behavior. Looking at colors affects our blood pressure, heartbeat, and respiration. Blue is calming, while yellow and red agitate the viewer. People frequently employ certain colors to achieve specific effects. For example, drunk tanks are often painted pink, because this seems to calm inmates' unruly behavior. Fast-food restaurants use a lot of orange and yellow in their marketing, because these colors have been shown to stimulate appetite. And suicides dropped 34 percent when London's Blackfriars Bridge was painted green (from black).

Even though colors seem to have universal meanings, we each have our own personal emotional responses to them. Regardless of your Colortype, finding a color you really respond to and keeping it nearby can provide a calming influence throughout the day.

Quiz: Discover Your Love Color

Look at each of these flowers and decide which one you're most attracted to. Don't judge your response to the photographs—just allow yourself to choose the one that makes you feel good.

Surprised by your favorite? Maybe you usually wear blues, but the yellow flower sent your heart aflutter? That flutter is telling you something—putting a little yellow into your wardrobe will surely lift your mood. Since love colors are for you, not meant to impress anyone else, you can find them secret hiding spots in any look you put together. Look for: jackets with bright linings, change purses, cocktail rings, cashmere gloves, and socks or tights.

If your love color can't be found on your Colortype palette, there's no need to break up with it. As long as you wear it as an accent to colors that flatter you, the affair can continue.

WHAT YOUR FAVORITE COLORS SAY ABOUT YOU

"THE COLORS WE ARE ATTRACTED TO SHIFT AS WE AGE," SAYS MICHELE BERNHARDT, PRACTITIONER OF THE INTUITIVE ARTS AND AUTHOR OF *COLORSTROLOGY*, A BOOK AND WEB SITE THAT ASSIGNS EVERYONE A COLOR BASED ON THEIR BIRTHDAY. "CHILDREN ARE ATTRACTED TO BRIGHT, INNOCENT COLORS, LIKE ORANGE AND RED, WHICH CONVEY ENTHUSIASM AND JOY."

Preferences shift toward darker colors and neutrals as people grow and take on more responsibility in the world, but not everyone's colors grow up. "You can tell so much about a person by what they are wearing," Bernhardt says. Here are her insights into what your color says about you:

ORANGE is about enthusiasm. It's energetic. It helps you move.

It's hard to wear **RED** or **BRIGHT ORANGE** and not do what you want. These are leadership colors. You cannot wear red unless you are going to step out. It conveys action, courage, assertiveness, and fearlessness.

NAVY BLUE people are discerning; they want it told like it is. They favor the color's crispness. They are using blue in an intellectual way.

LIGHTER BLUES are more expansive.

TURQUOISE BLUE is about vision. It's a travel color, for those constantly expanding their horizons.

It's very hard to get angry with somebody when they are wearing **LIGHT PINK**. It's a gentle color that will take away any feeling of aggression. Men are attracted to its femininity.

LIGHT BLUES are also good to increase gentleness.

GREENS can be grounding and health-oriented, like greens in nature. But they can also be associated with a focus on monetary success.

YELLOW can help you speak and think—it's about communication. Sunny colors are uplifting. They stimulate the mercurial side of our nature and make us mentally agile.

You won't see anyone who isn't spiritually inclined wearing **PURPLE**. Those who are closed-minded will not be attracted to it—it has a high vibration, especially the amethyst shade.

BLACK can be a foundation color, but I wouldn't recommend wearing it when you're feeling down. Black has an absorbing vibration, so it absorbs energy rather than reflecting it. It might provide a protective, insulating feeling, but it can't deflect negative feelings. If you're feeling down, put something light around your body—especially around your face.

WHITE is not easy to wear, because it carries the light and has a high vibration. But those who do wear it tend to be very spiritual.

EARTH TONES are very grounding.

NEUTRALS relay simplicity and humility.

And **METALLICS** remind us that we are special—and that life is full of wonder.

All this information about color can be useful when you'd like to convey specific messages or in situations where you need confidence. If you're giving a speech, for example, draw on the communicative powers of yellow. Going on a date? Try the male-luring draw of pale pink. Red would be the power choice for a TV appearance, while navy blue would work for a job interview in an analytical field. (Turquoise blue would better serve you in a creative interview.) Metallics are great mood-boosters on your down days, and neutrals are the right choice when you want to step back and let someone else take center stage—at your child's school play, for example.

FAVORITE COLORS OF THE FAMOUS

KATIE COURIC: *Cerulean*

What we say: Katie is a Sun, and cerulean is more of a Moon color. That said, she can certainly wear it as an accent—maybe in a fun summer tote.

COURTENEY COX: *Red*

What we say: Courteney, a classic Star, has chosen one of her most flattering hues. She should be sure to choose reds with blue undertones rather than yellow ones.

WHOOPI GOLDBERG: *Magenta*

What we say: Being an Earth, Whoopi is sure to look fantastic in the right magentas—deep, rich purple ones rather than those on the blue/pink side.

MOLLY SIMS: *Pastel purple*

What we say: Molly is a Sun, which means that her skin tone looks best in warm, golden colors. However, pastel purple is a very chic complement to grays, browns, and blacks—all colors on Molly's palette. She should look for a pastel purple cashmere sweater and layer it in with items in those colors.

CHRISTY TURLINGTON: *Green*

What we say: As an Earth, as well as an active environmentalist and yogi, Christy must be connecting to green on a spiritual level. Deep shades will flatter her, from forest to hunter.

JENNIFER CONNELLY: *Sea green*

What we say: The ultimate Star, Jennifer Connelly has chosen the right shade of green for her: The blue undertones in sea green connect to her black hair and match her eyes.

GWEN STEFANI: *Blue*

What we say: Although Gwen doesn't say which blue is her favorite, we'd put her in the iciest, lightest shade to play off her platinum hair, since the intense contrast between her dark eyes and platinum hair make her a Star.

ANGELINA JOLIE: *Black*

What we say: Big surprise, here, Angie. Can you imagine if the Goth goddess had said baby pink? Angelina used to wear black 24/7 but as she blossoms into an earth mother, she wears warm, flattering neutrals.

Color and the Red Carpet

Color sets a tone (pun intended). It brings a garment to life. Think of the different effects of a monochromatic Armani look versus a tight, bright multicolored dress from Roberto Cavalli. These looks send different messages, and most people's lives have room for both of them.

Back in the '90s, an Armani powersuit was the go-to look for the queens of the social and business worlds. Its somber tones and clean lines sent a message of quiet confidence. It's no wonder Hollywood studio heads and leading actresses were often photographed in this look—a neutral canvas really lets a woman's personality come to the forefront. But we like to think things have shifted a bit since the '90s—when powerful women once had to recede into the background visually speaking, not wanting to appear overly feminine, now they can show their true colors. Regardless, wear what makes you feel most confident.

A bright, printed, revealing dress is a frequent red-carpet choice these days, especially for ingenues new to the business. Making such a loud fashion statement can, ironically, take some pressure off the wearer—her dress is doing the talking for her, so it doesn't matter if she's tongue-tied!

VINTAGE AND COLOR

OUR FRIEND JULIANA CAIRONE OWNS AN AMAZING SHOWROOM CALLED RARE VINTAGE, WHICH IS SER-
ENDIPITOUSLY LOCATED NEXT TO OUR OFFICE. WE LOVE TO PEEK THROUGH HER GLASS DOORS EACH
MORNING TO GAZE UPON WHICHEVER GLORIOUS RELIC SHE HAPPENS TO BE DISPLAYING. WE ASKED HER
TO EXPLAIN THE CONNECTIONS BETWEEN SHOPPING VINTAGE AND WEARING COLOR.

The chicest celebrities come to Juliana for their red-carpet looks—she's the one responsible for putting Angelina Jolie in the museum-quality billowing brown Hermès gown she wore to the Screen Actors Guild in 2008. (Angelina, incidentally, is a Chic/Bohemian Earth—could this dress suit her Styletype any better?)

When you shop vintage, you don't have to rely upon the color palette of the season. There is a wider selection of colors and patterns to choose from, so it's always possible to express your individual style.

Certain designers are defined by their iconic use of color: Schiaparelli and shocking pink, Valentino and red, the jewel tones of Yves Saint Laurent.

Color reflects the American consumer's state of mind. During World War II, because of fabric rationing, the little black dress became a popular and practical item, while hats, which were not rationed, became elaborate and imaginative.

The postwar period of the 1950s brought a sense of relief and femininity, and women wore full skirts and pretty pastels. Christian Dior's famous "New Look" was luxurious and full of floaty, flowery prints.

Here is a 1950s skirt from Italian designer Gattinoni Sport.

The 1960s was the period of the space race and social upheaval. The Kennedys brought a feeling of sleek modernity to the White House. Mrs. Kennedy became an American fashion icon in her colorful suits and dresses. I remember in particular seeing at the Metropolitan Museum the red wool suit that she wore when giving the tour of the White House and the simple and sexy dresses in pinks and corals that she wore on holidays in Palm Beach and Capri. I think she was very aware of her image and realized that wearing color made her appear youthful and gave her an aura of enchantment.

This is a Roberto Capucci dress from the 1960s.

In the 1970s color was used to define Bohemian chic as explemified by the tie-dyes in greens and aqua of Halston and the romantic designs of Ossie Clark.

The 1980s were of course the time of power dressing and a display of cultural and economic excess. There was a lot of color in silks and satins and heavily jeweled pieces. The television show *Dynasty* probably best represents the period, with its deep purple, fuchsia, and red dresses usually lavishly bedecked in sequins, feathers, and just about anything else the costume designer, Nolan Miller, could think of.

Here is a 1970s Italian silk gown by La Mendola.

Check out this detail of a Patrick Kelly dress from the 1980s.

This is an Oscar de la Renta dress from the 1980s.

A LOT OF PASSION IS NECESSARY WHEN BUYING VINTAGE CLOTHES. IT IS ABOUT LOVE AND SOME-TIMES EVEN LUST. FOR A GRAND NIGHT OUT A GIRL MIGHT HAVE A VERY SPECIFIC IDEA OF WHAT IMAGE SHE WANTS TO PROJECT. SHE MIGHT WANT TO BE FULL-ON GLAMOROUS IN ICONIC VALENTINO RED; SHE MIGHT FEEL LIKE CHANNELING BIANCA JAGGER IN A SEXY WHITE YVES SAINT LAURENT PANTSUIT. PEOPLE SHOULD JUST FOLLOW THEIR OWN DESIRES AND BUY WHAT THEY LOVE.

COLORTYPE: **Earth**	STYLETYPE: **Whimsical**

SPRING/SUMMER SIGNATURE COLOR: **Hot Pink**

FALL/WINTER SIGNATURE COLOR: **Yellow**

Designer Lisa Perry is the talk of the town because her exhilarating mod dresses are inspired by the 1960s but totally wearable in the 2000s. Her aesthetic is clean, bright, and juicy, and her creations are like pieces of candy.

Here's Lisa on what's behind her colorful aesthetic:

I believe color affects people's moods. I witness the reaction daily when women are trying on my dresses or walk into my colorful studio or my home. They begin to smile and come alive in the presence of color. It lifts their mood. I also believe that color choices reflect a person's personality—serious vs. carefree; outgoing vs. reserved. When someone is willing to wear a bright color, they are saying, "Hello world, I am here, pay attention!"

I am inspired by the iconic designs of the 1960s, including fashion, pop, and minimal geometric art, furniture, architecture, and textiles. My favorite designers and artists include Pierre Cardin, Rudi Gernreich, André Courrèges, Saarinen, Mies van der Rohe, Marimekko, Joe Colombo, Verner Panton, Eames, Eero Aarnio, Roy Lichtenstein, Andy Warhol, and Alexander Liberman. Rather than saying what looks best, I like to help a woman find which color helps her to "come alive." I can tell right away if her face lights up and she smiles and feels comfortable in the color.

My earliest memory of color is the bright red "sit upon" I made in kindergarten—it was this little piece of padded cloth we took out of our cubbies at naptime! At age 10, my family lived in a house filled with color, including bright orange shag carpets in our den, and olive green and lemon yellow furniture and carpets in our living room. In the same house my dad painted my bedroom walls with swirls of yellow and orange to complement the bright yellow beads which hung in my doorway, of course!

This is a line-up of our hoop bags on display. They come in all colors of the rainbow and then some!

Here's Lisa in front of her display at Jeffrey New York, the downtown boutique frequented by the ultimate fashion insiders.

Lisa carries her design aesthetic into her own life, as you can see in this photo of her Palm Beach bedroom, which was inspired by the room she slept in as a child.

Here I am at my studio in one of my dresses. The dishes filled with M&Ms are a visitor's favorite.

What Image Do You Want to Project Today?

Of course, every woman wants to look great at all times, but sometimes a person needs to send a particular message. You can use specific colors to bring out certain elements of your personality and help you feel your best in all sorts of social situations.

For situations when you want to feel **CONFIDENT**, such as at a job interview or on a first date, we have three words: blue, blue, and blue. In a business situation, try a tailored shirt or sweater under a body-conscious jacket. When you're looking to connect with someone new, try a romantic blouse with jeans, or a luxurious scarf tossed over a T-shirt.

If you need to **STAND OUT**, red's your color. It draws attention, whether you're appearing on TV or giving a speech at your children's school benefit. For day, try layering a bright cashmere wrap over a turtleneck or T-shirt. For night, mix a knockout, fire-engine-bright piece in with your blacks. We love a red sequined tank worn with a tuxedo jacket and skinny pants.

When you're looking to project **SERENITY** and **POISE**—maybe you're throwing a holiday party or volunteering at a local charity—try head-to-toe ivories or whites. Jesse calls this look "creamy dreamy."

If you need to be perceived as **SMART** and **FOCUSED**, try charcoal. Whether you're attending a business dinner or your child's parent-teacher conference, dark gray reads as intelligent and appropriate. Try a charcoal blazer paired with a berry knit near your face and a pair of tailored, dark denim jeans for a classic, put-together look.

The Blue Trick

When we're feeling tired, nervous, or just generally down-in-the-dumps, we go to the closet and put on a blue shirt. We call this the "blue trick." Blue reminds us of the sky and the ocean, two endless expanses of beauty. Plus, the color seems to cool any redness in our faces—whether from a night out or a day in the Sun—and enhances the whites of our eyes. Blue is consistently the number one selling color at American specialty stores, so the rest of the world must be on to our trick. Consult your Colortype palette to find the right blue for you.

Here we are performing the blue trick. Notice how we both chose blues with a lot of green in them. Blues range from aquamarine to Tiffany to cerulean to midnight to sapphire, so you can surely find the perfect blue for you.

One of our favorite modern style icons is Michelle Obama. Here she is, gorgeous in her own perfect blue, with our friend (and designer of her delicious dress), Maria Pinto.

Color Breath

Many New Age healers believe colors have the power to heal. Teachers of Reiki, meditation, and biofeedback encourage their students to imagine breath filling their bodies with color. They use gemstones, prisms, lasers, fabrics, lenses, and bath additives to balance their clients' energies and recalibrate their auras. Whether you believe in holistic healing or not, color breathing can be a great tool for centering yourself before an important event, grabbing a moment when the kids are driving you crazy, or winding down before bed. Just close your eyes and, as you slowly inhale, imagine colorful light filling your body to its depths. Hold each breath for five seconds, then slowly exhale, repeating the process for 10 to 15 minutes.

Practitioners of color therapy assert that each color of the rainbow corresponds to one of the body's chakras and has the ability to affect the body and mind in different ways. Here is what chromo-therapists believe each different hue of "color breath" can bring.

COLOR	CHAKRA	BENEFITS
Red	Base *Spine*	Energizes, Stimulates appetite Boosts circulation
Orange	Sacral *Lower abdomen*	Encourages creativity, Brings self-respect, Warms
Yellow	Solar plexus *Below ribs*	Increases concentration, Encourages the intellect, Increases self-confidence
Green	Heart	Evokes love, Calms, Decreases stress
Blue	Throat	Encourages self-expression, Relaxes, Opens communication
Indigo	Third eye *Brow*	Develops intuition, Sedates, Opens the higher mind
Violet	Crown *Top of the head*	Helps with insomnia, Encourages spiritual awareness, Slows down frantic thinking

I like a very clean, put-together and sophisticated look. My style has evolved as I've matured–I was much more of a Chic/Whimsical in my 20s, but now I go for Chic and Chic/Avant-garde styles. In my 20s, I looked great as a dandy, with colorful pocket squares and ties. But moving into my 30s, this look began to seem costumey; now I feel more comfortable and sexier in Chic styles.

When you're very young, I think it's a great idea to experiment with Styletypes in the process of creating a fashion identity. For example, in seventh and eighth grades, the *Preppy Handbook* was my bible— and my love for pastel colors then may have marked the birth of the Whimsical side of me. Later, I took a break from preppy and at the beginning of college, I had a Goth moment! Once I realized life is not a music video—not all the time, any- way—I toned things down a bit. As our lives evolve, so does our style.

The common thread I've seen running through my early 20s until now is Chic. I go for pieces—jeans and jackets, for example—that are current and in style, but never trendy. I tend toward luxurious fabrics and modern lines, but I'm not neces- sarily into taking things over the fashion edge. Most important to me is fit. I think every garment should look bespoke—as though it were made just for you.

Some of my staple pieces—even the more fashion forward ones—tend to look classic on me since I have an All-American look. It takes an Avant-Garde piece to give me the edge I go for these days. I love a monochromatic look with a pop of color from the Moon palette—maybe an Adidas sneaker with a bright blue bottom, or a charcoal gray jacket with an eggplant lining.

I've always enjoyed helping friends and clients as they go through transitions in life and discover their own style identities. It's fun to be able to say, "I've been there."

My mother was no stranger to a round brush. I learned early in life that a haircut will take you everywhere. I loved that vest—I called it my suit, I felt so grown up in that. I was about three years old. My dad's color combo is all wrong—I wasn't a color expert at the time, and it shows. That jacket washes him out. The early '70s were all about earth tones—yes, we had a harvest gold refrigerator the color of my dad's tie.

That's my favorite haircut of all time. Before my mom was in accounting, she went to beauty school, so she knew how to cut hair. This red shirt is a little warm for me, but notice how it looks okay anyway, since the white collar is next to my face.

My nephew Quinn looks very similar to me when I was his age. But notice how he's a Sun, while I'm a Moon. I'd have to pay far too much for those highlights.

This is a photo of my last apartment, which was obviously decorated during my Chic/Whimsical stage. It's no accident that the bold blue walls just happened to be a perfect backdrop for my Colortype—a room needs to flatter its inhabitant!

I would never wear horizontal stripes again—they're definitely not slimming and they're not going to give me any height.

Kyoto inspired me—it is so peaceful and Zen. I love the look of the golden temple against nature.

Here I am in my late 20s, with my friend Annette in a metallic Hermés midnight blue shirt.

These are my doggies, Alex and Sacha, in the Hamptons. Hamptons grass in May is the most flattering backdrop for my children. Alex and Sacha are natural-born Stars. In winter months, their style is Chic, but they go nude in summer so I guess that makes them Bohemian!

COLOR AND YOUR HOME

WE BELIEVE PERKING UP YOUR HOME WITH COLOR IS JUST AS IMPORTANT AS USING IT TO PUNCH UP YOUR WARDROBE. JAMIE DRAKE, THE AUTHOR OF *JAMIE DRAKE'S NEW AMERICAN GLAMOUR*, IS ONE OF THE MOST TALENTED INTERIOR DESIGNERS WORKING TODAY. WE FIND HIS USE OF COLOR TOTALLY EXHILARATING AND INSPIRING. HERE, HE DESCRIBES THE FANTASY WOMEN WHO OCCUPY SOME OF HIS FAVORITE ROOMS—BY COLOR- AND STYLETYPE. SEE HOW YOUR FASHION SENSIBILITY INFLUENCES YOUR HOME IN THE GORGEOUS SPACES BELOW.

Color is essential to my interior design work. It is the first thing people notice when entering a space. It totally defines the mood and experience of a room. Being known as "the King of Color" within the interior design industry I do not limit myself to a signature color. I love to express myself with all colors available to me without the definition of a season. It is about being courageous, confident, playful and daring at all times throughout the year.

CHIC/CLASSIC MOON/EARTH

This room is definitely in the home of a Moon woman. It is cool and bewitching with a shiny silver moon ceiling. Yet this room is still rooted in the Earth—quite literally!—with a floor stained verdant mossy green and accents of apple green throughout the room. The woman who lives in this room is totally Chic, with a soupçon of the Classic (witness the riding trophy lamp, the cushiony chaise longue . . .).

CLASSIC/CHIC SUN/EARTH

This is the sitting room of a complex personality. It's a mix of Sun and Earth, yin and yang. A glacier white floor and columns, soft leaf walls, and coal black furniture are set off by the fiery, intense coral pillows and ceiling. A true Classic (Ionic pilasters, marble floor, antiques), yet Chic (a mirror-legged sofa, retro-modern table and cabinet), the woman who lives in this room proves herself complex and sophisticated.

BOHEMIAN/AVANT-GARDE STAR

A real Star, the occupant of this room sparkles vibrantly at all times, and the design reflects it. Doses of turquoise, light shattering on glass, twinkling surfaces of silver leaf and crackled mirror, this room reflects the essence of the famed endless summer nights of Russia, the White Nights. The mix of pieces, fur rug, and collection of accessories define it as a downtown diva's Bohemian/Avant-Garde lair.

CHIC/BOHEMIAN SUN

A type-A woman, with a thousand-megawatt Sun personality, would be quite at home in this room (even though it's my own bedroom!). Because of the strong yellows throughout, it is bathed in high noon 24/7. Chic, certainment, mon cher! But also Bohemian, with all those animals prints strewn about. Out of Africa? No, out of this world!

Makeup faux pas are easy to avoid when you *understand your undertones.*

CHAPTER 8
COLOR AND MAKEUP

W e asked our friend Darcy McGrath, who did all the makeup in this book and has worked with icons in media and entertainment such as Oprah and Cate Blanchett, to discuss how to determine the best makeup colors for your complexion.

Finding Your Makeup Colors (and Keeping It Natural)

The colors of your makeup impact the way your skin looks even more than the clothes you wear. (Sorry, Jesse and Joe!) Have you ever bought a bag of cosmetics after having a department store makeover and then gone home only to realize you look like one of the stars of *The Golden Girls*: 20 years older than you are and totally '80s? You can't trust those fluorescent lights in the perfume department, or trendy, seasonal color stories driven more by marketing than flattery.

When makeup goes wrong, it goes *very* wrong. Foundation intended to smooth skin becomes masklike. Eye colors meant to cast a flattering shadow instead shroud eyes in exhausted darkness. Lipstick that was supposed to create a full, sumptuous mouth bleeds into lip lines, making you look like you've been drinking tomato soup out of a teacup.

I once heard a story about a friend's child who, when saying goodbye to her mom as she left for an elegant evening event, said, "Mommy, you look so pretty, but you don't look like my mommy."

Makeup faux pas are easy to avoid when you understand your undertones and how to blend and layer your makeup. Jesse and Joe have already done the hard work by helping you determine your Colortype. I asked some of my model friends to pose for before-and-after shots demonstrating the most common mistakes women make in choosing makeup colors. It's smooth sailing from here; just find your Colortype in the following pages to discover your best (and worst) makeup colors.

SUN

Wrong color: **Blue-red**

Loretta has all the golden glory of a true Sun, but by wearing the wrong shade of foundation and a shade of lipstick that fights her undertones, she masks her true colors and ages her look.

SKIN

By matting her skin, Loretta is committing the number one sin of makeup application for women over 40: too much powder. When you're older, you want the moisture in your skin to show, not to get absorbed by a bunch of complexion-covering molecules.

EYES

The black liner close to her lash line makes her eyes look tired, and that's a major no-no in our over-caffeinated society, where everyone's number one priority is looking awake. Looking tired is very aging. You want to convey, "I'm healthy. I work out. My glow is earned!"

LIPS

Because Loretta has golden undertones, this bluish lipstick looks really harsh. She's already striking and angular—she doesn't need to intensify it with a high-drama look.

CHEEKS

Often, the tip with blush is to attempt to create a youthful glow with pink cheeks, but the wearer ends up looking theatrical.

Right Color: **Apricot**

SKIN
With much less foundation, and a light dusting of bronzer replacing the translucent powder that masked her natural radiance in the "Before" photo, Loretta loses 10 years.

EYES
Golden tones play up the size of her eyes and the strength of her brow bones.

LIPS
A soft apricot gloss is much more feminine and flattering than high-impact lipstick.

CHEEKS
Creamy apricot blush shows off her tan.

SUN Best Colors	Stay Away From . . .
EYES: Apricot, peach, gold, copper	Purple, berry, gray
LIPS: Apricot, warm rose	Blue-red, dark brown
CHEEKS: Apricot, warm bronze	Blue-pink

☾ MOON

Wrong color: Orange

Find me a woman who looks good in orange eye shadow. I'm sure she exists, but she's as rare as a unicorn.

SKIN

See how the wrong makeup colors actually make her complexion appear to change from her face to her neck and chest?

EYES

Orange can be aging on the wrong complexion, and here, it makes Jovanka—a young mom—look tired. Matching the frosty orange shadow to the pale orange lipstick is a sin many women commit: It's a monochromatic no-no.

LIPS

The lipstick finish looks dated: It's pearlized, high-pigment, and entirely too high-drama for carpool.

CHEEKS

What are people thinking when they apply a shade of blush that doesn't occur naturally?

Right color: Berry

Here, I worked with Jovanka's natural undertone, which is pink.

SKIN

A soft finish shows off her lovely porcelain complexion.

EYES

I kept her eye makeup very light—just a little dusting of ivory shadow on her lids to even them out—and finished her off with black mascara on the top and bottom lashes.

LIPS

A soft berry pink is expressed with intensity here. It's a very romantic look but not too severe because it matches her undertones.

CHEEKS

I applied a rose-colored cream-on blusher underneath a light foundation, so the color on her cheeks looks as though it's coming from within.

MOON Best Colors	Stay Away From . . .
EYES: Rose, silver, cool shimmering brown	Orange, bronze
LIPS: Blue-red, hot pink, cool rose	Tomato red, lilac
CHEEKS: Cherry stain, English rose	Peach, dark brown, shimmering orange

EARTH

Wrong color: **Mauve**

This mauve palette is not appropriate for Eleanor's skin—it looks unnatural. Her dusty violet eye shadow and pale, coral-pink lip color are popular among women who think pastels make them look younger, but in reality these colors just make you look faded—especially when they are not harmonious with your skin tone.

SKIN

By now, you know what I'm going to say. The wrong foundation can have a masking effect.

EYES

See the way bags appear under her eyes? So often, women want to conceal these, but when they apply concealer in too light a shade, it ends up appearing chalky, heavy, and dry—thus calling more attention to the problem. To fix this common mistake, think dark to light. Apply your foundation first, which will conceal the bags. Then apply a small fingertip's worth of light concealer on top of the foundation to smooth and balance your eye.

LIPS

You'll know a bad lip color when it makes the color of your gums and your teeth seem off. Match your lip color to your gums, and you'll never go wrong. After all, your lip color needs to make your mouth and teeth look great. Since this color fights Eleanor's undertones, it will make her teeth look yellow and her look dated.

CHEEKS

When there's too much white in a blush color, as there is in the mauve shade Eleanor wears here, it can appear chalky on deeper skin tones.

Right color: **Raisin**

Eleanor comes alive in raisin lip and cheek color, accented with gold and warm bronze.

SKIN

To enhance the natural curves all over her face I applied a little powder highlight on her cheekbones and the sides of her nose.

EYES

Black mascara and eyeliner thicken and elongate her natural lashes. On her lids, I used a soft brown shimmer shadow to enhance the shape of her eyes. On top of the shimmer brown, I used a golden brown to highlight her brow bones and draw out her lower lashline. To open up Asian eyes, turn the corners up a little with luminescent shadow.

LIPS

The depth of her lip color gives her a brightness that works for day or evening. I made sure to apply some clear gloss over the deep color on her lips—this keeps the look young and moist.

CHEEKS

I used a golden, earthy brown blusher and topped it with a deep bronze powder.

EARTH Best Colors	Stay Away From . . .
EYES: Raisin, eggplant, warm brown, golden brown	Sky blue, yellow, pink
LIPS: Raisin, deep berry, warm brown	Fuchsia, blue-red, rose-pink
CHEEKS: Warm peach, bronze	Peony pink, red stain

STAR

Wrong color: Pale peach

Often, when someone is trying to achieve a soft and "natural" look, they go paler than their natural skin tone, and all this does is call attention to the makeup instead of the person.

SKIN

Samantha has olive skin and cool undertones. But there is a golden element to her skin, which has to be addressed, too. People often try to mask their overall look with just one foundation color. This is the primary difference between makeup that's been done professionally and the way women do their makeup at home: Many women are afraid to mix colors, but pros know that mixing colors is the key to achieving a natural result. My favorite "mixing" tip is actually a bit of a cheat: Layer a warm shade of powder bronzer over a foundation that matches your untanned skin. This adds depth and appears to give skin a realistic flush. Concentrate the bronzer on the high planes of the face—the cheekbones, the bridge of the nose, and the forehead—these are the areas where the sun naturally hits.

EYES

Golden shadow makes her eyes look smaller than they are.

LIPS

Going orangey and golden will take away from the color of her teeth—making them look yellow, when they are actually white and vibrant.

CHEEKS

Powder blush in the ever-popular pale peach color doesn't heighten or brighten her skin, which is what makeup should do. Instead, it makes her look sickly.

Right color: Pomegranate

Now, Samantha has a radiant, healthy glow.

SKIN

I brightened her face by addressing both her cool and warm tones. I used a combination of a warmer foundation and a cooler blusher, then went over both with a powder bronzer. The final veil of bronzer is a key element—it creates harmony among all the colors on her face.

EYES

Aside from mascara and a little black eyeliner, I kept the eye makeup light so her lips could take center stage.

LIPS

I wanted to go a bit dramatic with Samantha's lip color because Stars can carry off drama, I used a deep red with a clear gloss on top. This dark blue-red draws attention to the whites of her eyes and her natural luminosity, and enhances her natural hair color.

CHEEKS

Use a cool damp sponge to tap a cool cream blusher into the apples of your cheeks first, then go over it lightly with a warm foundation. Finish the look with a sweep of powder blush in a shade that reflects the cream blusher.

STAR Best Colors	Stay Away From . . .
EYES: White shimmer, dark gray, ice blue	Warm brown, warm peach
LIPS: Blue-red, magenta, light pink	Brown, coral, dusty rose
CHEEKS: Red stain, wine stain	Apricot, warm bronzer

DON'T FORGET YOUR EYEBROWS!

THE SHAPE AND DEFINITION OF YOUR EYEBROWS ARE JUST AS IMPORTANT AS ANY COLOR YOU PUT ON YOUR FACE. WHETHER OR NOT YOU PLAN TO WEAR MAKEUP, YOU MUST GROOM YOUR EYEBROWS, BECAUSE THEY PROVIDE A FRAME OF REFERENCE FOR YOUR FACE.

To make the most of your brows, visit a brow specialist for a consultation, even if you don't plan to maintain them professionally. He or she will be able to explain the best shape for your face and teach you proper plucking technique. If you have sparse brows, fill them in and define them with a pencil, then softly layer a powder one shade lighter than your natural color on top, for soft definition. Go for a color a shade lighter than your hair—too dark can look garish. Use small upward brushstrokes, mimicking hair growth, for invisible brow support.

PREPPING THE CANVAS

NONE OF THESE "AFTERS" WOULD BE POSSIBLE WITHOUT THE RIGHT SKIN CARE UNDERNEATH. YOU NEED A VERY HYDRATING MOISTURIZER TO PROVIDE AN OCCLUSIVE LAYER FOR YOUR SKIN, PROTECTING IT FROM THE ELEMENTS AND ALLOWING MAKEUP TO ADHERE. THIS LAYER WILL HOLD YOUR FOUNDATION IN PLACE AND KEEP YOUR MAKEUP FROM FADING THROUGHOUT THE DAY.

You can also apply hydration all day long, without disturbing your makeup, by using a protein mist (Epicuren makes a great one). It will feel refreshing, and it reactivates the pigments and finishes of the colors you've put on your face without disturbing the finish. It also helps to make the makeup look as though it's your skin.

There's a common misconception that women with oily skin don't need to moisturize. Our bodies can actually overproduce oil when our skin is not well hydrated. This oil will make the face appear shiny and can change the look of makeup over the course of the day, because when sebum oxidizes, it turns yellow. This is why people with oily skin develop a yellow cast when they use the wrong skin care or wear pore-clogging makeup. Blotting papers without powder are great to take care of extra oil; try using a colorless pressed powder or mineral makeup to give your skin a pretty, matte finish.

THE STYLETYPES AND MAKEUP

JUST AS DIFFERENT STYLETYPES EXPRESS THEMSELVES DIFFERENTLY THROUGH THEIR CLOTHING CHOICES, THEY ALSO SHOW THEIR TASTES THROUGH MAKEUP. HERE ARE THE QUINTESSENTIAL LOOKS FOR EACH STYLE TYPE:

STYLETYPE: Classic

DAYTIME MAKEUP SIGNATURE: Sunny bronzer
The Classic woman wants to look like she's been out horseback riding all day. For the most natural, youthful look, choose a bronzer with a soft shimmer, or a creamy blush with a slightly brick-red cast so the complexion looks invigorated, not streaky.

NIGHTTIME MAKEUP SIGNATURE: Red lips
Where better to take your beauty cues than from glamorous old movies? The key to giving your red serious staying power is blotting between two to three coats. Check out your Colortype makeup chart to find your best red. Choose the formula and finish you prefer, from tint to stain, creamy to matte.

STYLETYPE: Chic

DAYTIME MAKEUP SIGNATURE: Glowing skin
Confidence is great skin. But you can fake it till you make it: Just moisturize for a dewy finish, then tap foundation only into red or discolored areas. Finish with a loose, illuminating powder to reflect light off the face.

NIGHTTIME MAKEUP SIGNATURE: Shimmering shadow
The Chic woman's nighttime makeup strategy is an extension of her day look: Blending some shimmery, neutral shadow into the creases of the eyelids will give eyes depth and subtly enhance them.

STYLETYPE: Bohemian

DAYTIME MAKEUP SIGNATURE: Kohl eyeliner
Remember that cool girl in high school, the one who looked like she only took her makeup off every other day? Get her cool factor with a soft eyeliner pencil (black if you're a brunette, brown if you're a blonde or a redhead) blended into the lashline all around your eyes. If your eyes are on the small side, stick to the top lashline only.

NIGHTTIME MAKEUP SIGNATURE: Smoked-out eyes
For a night out, the Bohemian needs only to add some deep shadow (see your Colortype makeup chart for color suggestions) on top of her eyeliner, then use a soft brush to blend it up and out from the upper lashline.

STYLETYPE: Whimsical

DAYTIME MAKEUP SIGNATURE: Candy apple blush
Nothing's easier, girlier, or happier than a pop of bright blush on the apples of cheeks. The Whimsical needs nothing else to create a signature daytime look.

NIGHTTIME MAKEUP SIGNATURE: Major lashes
Remember that iconic photo of Twiggy in which her eyelashes fanned out like rays of the sun? We're not saying you should go that dramatic, but layering multiple coats of mascara on well-curled lashes will open up your eyes like nothing else.

STYLETYPE: Avant-Garde

DAYTIME MAKEUP SIGNATURE: Liquid liner
It can be tough to master at first, but the Avant-Garde woman likes a challenge. Liquid liner makes a strong, geometric statement, just like an Avant-Garde wardrobe. Black is classic, but dark colors like plums, blues, and greens look cool, too.

NIGHTTIME MAKEUP SIGNATURE: High-impact lipstick
Ever notice how there's always one or two "crazy" shades of lipstick in every seasonal makeup collection? From Day-Glo pink to blood red, these extreme colors are made for fashion risk-takers. Try them with a naked face for maximum impact, or as a stain for a more subtle look (just apply and blot a few times so the color stains your lips while highlighting your natural skin tone).

COLORTYPE: **Sun**   STYLETYPE: **Chic/Classic**

SPRING/SUMMER SIGNATURE COLOR: **Moss Green**

FALL/WINTER SIGNATURE COLOR: **Bright Orange**

Tracey Kemble is a true inspiration. Not just because of her beauty, or her poise, or her stellar career as a film executive—but also because she is a survivor. Tracey was in a terrible accident and had to relearn to walk and talk, and now she's doing it with more grace than ever.

I have always been attracted to color—the brighter and bolder, the better for me. I go toward bold oranges, greens, and pinks. I never think about it when I shop, but clearly there's a theme.

My family is from Jamaica, and my childhood was filled with tropical plants and flowers. My cousins in Jamaica wore bright yellow hotpants—anything went! If you saw their shirts and tops lying on the bed together, you would say, "absolutely not," but somehow everything worked once they put it on.

Color makes me happy. It makes me feel alive.

My apartment before I got married was your typical West Village fifth-floor walkup—and the most colorful place in the world, to me. It had every color under the sun: the bedroom was Tuscan orange, the living room was mustard gold, the kitchen was Carribbean green—the palette exploded. I wanted something warm, cozy, and vibrant, but I didn't want it to feel like I spent a lot of

My mother has a very colorful personality! One of my favorite photos of her is in a yellow, green, and lavender Pucci print. She always told me to value quality above quantity—5 beautifully crafted pieces are better than 20 just-okay ones.

time picking out colors. After people caught their breath from walking up five floors, the color was so soothing. We would make tea on my grandmother's china, sprawl on the couch, and sleep. It wasn't big, but I treated it like a palace.

My married apartment was designed by the people who did the Calvin Klein and Donna Karan stores—very modern and cool, with crisp colors and lines. It's 10 different colors from a natural palette—beige, light gray, khaki—and it's stunning, but it's the opposite of me!

I lean toward a strong version of lilac—a deep, deep purple—and Tuscan orange. I love wearing color, but I don't like fussiness. I usually prefer solids to prints and stripes. I can have fun with color when the style is streamlined.

This is me with Jesse trying on a fabulous red trench. We always have such a great time together.

This blue dress made me feel magical. I just loved the way this dress was absolutely effortless. I didn't have to fit in a mold—it just felt like me. I was literally floating.

Your hair color
brings light to your face.

CHAPTER 9
HAIR AND COLOR

Even in flawless makeup and a drop-dead fabulous ensemble, a woman cannot look put-together without the right hair color. Your hair color is what brings light to your face—the right one can brighten your skin and eyes, the wrong one can make you disappear. In this chapter, a few of our favorite hair gurus break down how to make your hair work for you.

Our friend Stephen Knoll has owned one of the top salons in New York City for more than 15 years. He has worked with countless celebrities, including Ashley Judd, Cindy Crawford, Debra Messing, and Maria Shriver. Women love him because he doesn't believe in one-size-fits-all trends but in creating a unique look tailored to each woman's individual beauty. Here are his philosophies on hair color:

If you're contemplating a big change, but you're not sure you're ready, try on some wigs. Make sure they're made of human hair because synthetic fibers won't catch the light the way your hair does. If you find one you like, bring it to your colorist for a perfect match.

Warmer tones are typically better than ashy shades for most people. The warmer tones are softer and easier to maintain. Of course, there are people who look best in cool tones—often, the very old or the very young. What you want to avoid is looking washed-out, which typically means you don't have enough contrast between your hair and your skin. The one exception to this rule is with platinum blondes like Gwen Stefani and Gwyneth Paltrow. Gwen pulls her look off by wearing intense makeup—creating contrast and interest around her eyes and lips with black eyeliner and red lipstick. Gwyneth's hair color suits her Chic/Bohemian style, but when she goes without makeup, she has to beware of looking too washed-out, since her complexion, eyes, and hair are all so pale.

Don't go too extreme. Often, women who dye their hair for the first time choose colors that are too dark or too red. For the most part, subtler is better. There are, of course, wonderful exceptions, like Lucille Ball, Marilyn Monroe, and Diana Vreeland. Each of these women's looks were defined by her hair color and perfectly suited to her personality.

There's no rule saying your hair color needs to get lighter as you get older. Remember, the key is how your hair color makes your skin look. Your hair is a frame for your face. Think of Susan Sarandon's deep auburn against her golden skin, or Isabella Rossellini's near-black bob against her pale jaw.

Your stylist can come up with the most brilliant look in the world, but if you're taken out of your comfort zone, if you're not empowered, you can't carry it off.

Hair-Color Glossary: What You Need to Know

Single-process color lifts pigment from your hair and deposits a new color using just one formula. It is used when you want to go no more than a few shades lighter or darker than your natural hair color.

Semipermanent color is a single-process solution that can be used at home to darken or deepen your natural hair color. It washes out after 6–8 weeks.

Double-process color is used by professionals to perform drastic changes. First, the hair is stripped of all its natural color; then, it is "toned" with a new shade.

Highlighting involves bleaching sections of hair—either using foils or a palette and paintbrush—to create dimension.

Low-lighting involves adding darker sections to previously lightened hair in order to create contrast.

Brassiness is a word used to describe hair that looks orange or yellowish after it's been colored. Usually brassiness is the product of oxidation—when hair color is inadvertently lifted or corrupted by sunlight, chlorine, or overly aggressive shampoo. Avoid oxidation by using shampoo, conditioner, and even sun-protection formulated especially for color-treated hair.

"My real hair color is kind of a dark blonde. Now I just have mood hair." —Julia Roberts, *actress*

Louis Licari's Hair-Color Words to Live By

Louis Licari is internationally known as the king of hair color. He has salons in New York City and Beverly Hills and has changed the locks of almost any gorgeous celebrity you can think of. He was trained as a painter, so he takes an artistic view of hair color. Here are his fail-safe words of wisdom:

If you have the coloring of a brunette and want to go blonder, leave some depth at your roots and make the tips of your hair lighter. Keep your eyebrows their natural color. This will allow you to make your hair color light and still complement your complexion. Think Sarah Jessica Parker or Gisele Bündchen—they have beachy highlights that start a few inches from their parts. Stay within a few shades of your natural color. This is the perfect way to make sure your new color complements your skin tone.

If you have to wear more makeup to make your new hair color work, you have picked the wrong color. If you stay within your own color range, touch-ups will be less frequent.

Red undertones can help every color to come alive and make you look prettier. Think about the difference between an ash blonde and a golden blonde or an ash brown and a chocolate brown. Ash colors are drab and drain the color from your complexion. Warm (red) base colors make your skin color come alive. Hair color should brighten your look. When you have the right hair color, it should look like you have on a bit of makeup.

People with sallow complexions—those with yellow undertones who look sickly without a touch of sun—must avoid lighter warm shades. They will blend with your skin color and make your skin appear more sallow. This is a major beauty faux pas. You should choose a darker color to provide contrast with your skin color. Dark golden blondes, deep chocolates, and dark auburns work best with sallow complexions.

Semipermanent colors can appear darker and more opaque than their color descriptions. Always color a few strands of hair at the nape of your neck before you apply color to your entire head. This will allow you to see your new color and avoid any surprise endings.

Don't go too blonde if you are pale. Your face will blend with your hair color and you will disappear. Contrast is the key to looking vital.

THE POWER OF HIGHLIGHTS

AN EASY WAY TO CREATE DIMENSION IN THE HAIR—WITHOUT DEPOSITING ANY COLOR PIGMENTS—IS BY ADDING SUBTLE BLEACH HIGHLIGHTS. CHRISTOPHER BOZARTH, OWNER AND COLORIST AT CHICAGO'S 2109 DIVISION SALON, EXPLAINS WHAT TO ASK FOR:

Redheads lose luster as they age because, as they spend less time outside, their hair is exposed less frequently to the elements. Since the lightening power of the Sun is what reveals the hair's underlying pigments, the hair can become dark and flat. To recreate what the Sun used to do, redheads should replicate what would happen on vacation by asking for a few foil highlights around the face, at the crown, and at the part—all places where the Sun would naturally hit.

Ask for: Golden and strawberry blonde highlights. Stay within a few shades of your natural color to avoid a dated, skunky look.

Brunettes can go two ways with their highlights—golden blonde if the natural hair color is on the light side, or red tones if the natural color is very dark. The most important thing for brown-haired girls to remember is that ashy (meaning cool) highlights never look natural.

Ask for: Golden blonde and red highlights.

Blondes almost always need to lighten their hair as they get older. Pale but buttery highlights will restore the luster to most blondes' locks. Even the lightest blonde should be wary of ashy tones—pale streaks should be more buttery than white or silver, which will look frosted and gray.

Ask for: Pale, warm, blonde highlights.

YOUR STYLETYPE AND YOUR HAIRSTYLE

IT HAS BEEN SAID MANY TIMES THAT YOUR HAIR IS YOUR BEST ACCESSORY, AND WHILE IT PAINS US TO RELEGATE A CROCODILE BIRKIN BAG OR LIZARD LOUBOUTIN SLING BACKS TO SECOND PLACE, WE AGREE. WHILE THE MOST IMPORTANT CONSIDERATION IN CHOOSING A HAIRSTYLE IS THAT IT FLATTERS YOUR FACE, YOUR HAIRSTYLE IS ALSO AN IDEAL CHANNEL THROUGH WHICH TO EXPRESS YOUR STYLETYPE.

Here are each Styletype's quintessential looks:

Classic
SHORT:

The blunt bob, *Kate Bosworth*

Classic
LONG:

Shiny layers, *Jamie King*

Chic

SHORT:

The graduated bob, *Katie Holmes*

Chic

LONG:

Sleek and straight, *Angie Harmon*

Whimsical
SHORT:

Louise Brooks bob, *Christina Ricci*

Bohemian
SHORT:

The soft crop, *Michelle Williams*

Whimsical
LONG:

Heavy bangs, *Camilla Bell*

Avant-Garde

SHORT:

The punky boy cut, *Rihanna*

Bohemian

LONG:

Loose, layered waves, *models backstage at a fashion show*

Avant-Garde

LONG:

Longer-in-the-front, *Leigh Lezark of the Misshapes*

CHAPTER 10
ANY QUESTIONS?

There are always questions. Here are some of the best we've heard:

I'm considering changing my hair color somewhat noticeably. Will I have to rethink my entire wardrobe to match?

Hopefully, you're choosing your new hair color wisely. Remember that it will look best if it's within a few shades of your natural color. Assuming you're staying within the palette you were born with, you shouldn't have to replace your whole wardrobe. The neutrals that flatter you will stay the same as your hair color changes. You should, however, reexamine the pop pieces you wear near your face—scarves, sweaters, and T-shirts, for example. If you're deepening your hair color, you might want to invest in some deeper pops—and vice versa. For example, a strawberry blonde who's going deep auburn might trade her pale blue scarves for deep teal ones in order to balance the intensity of her hair color. And a golden blonde who's going platinum will be amazed at how intense everything looks next to her hair once it's nearly white. She'll need to trade in her newly harsh sweaters for gentler tones.

I love wearing navy and brown, but I hate always having to wear matching shoes and bag, et cetera. What can I do to make the accessories I have more versatile across color palettes?

First of all, navy shoes are only for flight attendants! (Unless they are crushed velvet and you're wearing them with a Galliano gown to the Costume Institute gala.) It's true that certain colors, like navy, browns, and certain neutrals, look better with accessories that aren't black. To pair with browns and neutrals, we love shoes and bags made from the deepest brown leather you can find. Layering different shades of brown looks rich and sophisticated, so there is no need to make sure your shoes and bag match. The best accessories to wear with navy depend on your Styletype. Classic Styletypes should go for cordovan or rich chocolate in the cooler seasons, and brown sandals come summertime. Chics and Bohemians can try the Classic choices, or explore metallics (both silver and gold look killer with navy). For Whimsicals, anything goes: red for a fun, vintage-inspired look, white during spring and summer days when you want to be super fashionable.

Is there a shoe color that every wardrobe MUST have, aside from the basic black and brown, of course?

When it comes to accessories, metallics are the new neutrals. No matter what your Style- or Colortype, there is a metallic for you. In general, people who have mostly warm colors in their wardrobes (that's you, Sun and Earth), do well with gold or bronze, and people with mostly cool colors in their wardrobes look great in pewter and silver. Our two fave metallic shoe styles are ballet flats in soft kidskin and strappy sandals with a high heel for an evening out.

Do I have to match my handbag to my shoes and gloves?

This question makes us shudder with visions of Queen Elizabeth. Please, don't ever match your handbag, shoes, and gloves to one another, unless you're an extra in a 1950s movie. Accessories should coordinate, not match. What do we mean? Keep things in the same color family, but mix up textures and materials. Some examples: Try a pair of brown riding boots with a deep burgundy messenger bag and camel cashmere gloves, or red ballet flats with a black suede tote and black kidskin gloves.

Is it true that if you want to dye your hair, you would look best with the color you had as a child?

Opinions differ on this one. Louis Licari says you can't go wrong with a color you've already worn; Stephen Knoll says sometimes you're not born with your best color, and you should go for whichever shade you feel best in. We think it comes down to lifestyle: If you're low-maintenance but want to punch up your look, get highlights or a semipermanent tint that harks back to your childhood hair color. If you're a diva who doesn't care how much time you have to spend in root touch-ups as long as you look like a bombshell, by all means go from black to platinum. Just be sure your new color doesn't clash with your skin tone, and adjust makeup accordingly.

In the summer, my skin naturally tans, does this mean I should adjust my wardrobe colors seasonally?

Not consciously. The marketplace will affect this adjustment for you. The colors stores offer in spring and summer come in much softer and lighter colors than those they offer in the cooler seasons. And chances are, when it's 90 degrees outside, you're more likely to reach for your white jeans than your black ones, since dark colors absorb heat. A better way to think about adjusting your wardrobe seasonally is to make sure you're choosing appropriate fabrics. We like natural fibers year-round, but cotton and linen are especially key in summertime, when your skin needs to breathe to stay cool. Save wools and synthetics—which usually come in darker colors, incidentally—for fall and winter. Denim, twill, and canvas work well any time of year.

I'm a bridesmaid for my sister. I look best in tawny colors. She's chosen baby blue for the dresses. What can I do so I don't look awful in the wedding photos?

Is a wheat-colored pashmina an option? If not, we've got two words for you: big hair. Your hair is (hopefully) a color that flatters you, and it's the best possible frame for your face. Wear it down at the wedding. If you've got your heart set on an updo, so much can be done with makeup. We don't normally advocate changing your skin tone with makeup, but a makeup artist can tone down your natural warmth with powder and blush. An allover luminizer on arms, neck, and décolletage can do wonders to brighten skin when it's stuck in an unflattering color.

For my wedding, I really want to wear a virginal white gown, but I've always been told that white washes me out. What can I do?

Wedding dresses come in an array of "white" shades, such as antique ivory, ecru, tea-stained beige, and blush. Ladies with warm skin tones look gorgeous in yellow-tinged whites, and those with cool skin tones should go for pale pinks, pure whites, and even lighter-than-light blues and grays. Work with what flatters you—as long as your gown is monochromatic and lighter than khaki, no one will mistake you for a bridesmaid when you walk down that aisle.

I've always heard that you should wear colors that match your eyes. My eyes are aqua, but I feel ridiculous in that color. Can I just wear plain old blue?

You can wear any shade of blue—or green, for that matter. Both of these will enhance your aqua irises and make the whites of your eyes pop. Beware of icy, pale blue if you are a warm skin tone (Sun or Earth)—it will make you look sallow. Stick to the shades on your Colortype palette.

What colors are best for bathing suits when your skin is very pale?

Avoid very light colors, because you don't want to appear ghostly on the beach. Black, though, can seem a bit harsh against porcelain skin. Try navy blue, chocolate, or jewel tones—which work especially well for the Star Colortype.

What colors are best for bathing suits to slim the hips/make me look skinny/make my chest look bigger or smaller?

See, aren't you glad you learned about color theory? Yellow is the most visible of all the colors in the spectrum, so wear it on the parts of your body you want to emphasize. Same goes for red and white. Black and blue absorb more light, so they're more slimming. So many bathing separates are available today that it's really easy to create a custom-colored suit. If you want to make your chest look larger and minimize your hips, try a red bikini top with a black bottom. If you're looking to slim your tummy and play up your bottom, try a navy blue tankini top with red boy shorts. And if you prefer a one-piece, look for solid, dark colors with interest around the décolletage—this look flatters every body type. Conversely, bright, big-printed maillots can make a size 4 look like a size 14. You're better off in a beach towel.

Are there some neutrals that aren't right for everyone?

We prefer to say that everyone has a set of neutrals that will flatter them. Certainly the warm khaki that looks great on a dark-skinned Earth can make a fair-skinned Sun look ill. That said, certain neutrals are particularly difficult to wear, no matter what your Colortype. Despite its status as a classic, camel is very difficult to wear. There's a reason racks of "classic" camel coats are always on sale. Same goes for oatmeal, stone, and grayish beige, which tend to wash everyone out, especially if they are worn without a pop piece. Remember that the key to finding a flattering neutral is making sure it contrasts with your natural skin tone.

What colors are best during pregnancy—both to make you look slim and to make your face look aglow?

Your Colortype won't change when you go through a pregnancy, so stick to the colors on your palette. What you should consider, though, is keeping a long, clean line. Monochromatic looks will look great on you. And don't be afraid to show off your fertile form in body-conscious shapes. There are great fashion-conscious maternity lines available at every price point, from A Pea in the Pod to Liz Lange for Target.

How do I choose the best shade of nail polish?

Nail polish is one place you can really have fun, all rules be damned! It's the best place to try out the hot color of the season—from fluorescent pink to midnight blue—even when it's not on your palette. Some nail colors may be inappropriate for certain situations (bright red can send the wrong message in a conservative work environment), so use your discretion.

Any tips for the guy in my life? How do I get him to stop wearing just black, brown, and blue?

Men belong to the same Colortypes as women, so have your guy take the quiz! Get him set up with a foundation of neutrals that suit him, and then have fun with pop colors. Ties and pocket squares are a great way to get even the most conservative guy to love color. Patterned shirts that mix neutrals and colors are great, too, provided they accentuate his best features. If he is tall and slim, windowpane and plaid patterns are masculine and fun. If he is of a thicker build, stick to vertical stripes in darker tones. And encourage him to get some brown shoes, and a charcoal jacket—great alternatives to black that flatter everyone.

How can I use color to make me seem taller (or shorter)?

To appear taller, go monochromatic. Don't cut your midsection in half by wearing different colors on top and bottom, and if you're wearing a belt, make sure it blends into your pants or skirt. You'll want to create a column of color. If you want to minimize your height (why anyone would want to do such a thing, we don't know!), try wearing a light color on top and a darker one on the bottom, or vice versa. Cutting your silhouette in half will break up a tall appearance.

I have naturally rosy cheeks, what are the best colors to wear to tone down the redness in my complexion?

Makeup artists use green to counteract red on the skin, but the same trick doesn't necessarily work when it comes to clothing. When you want to come across cool and collected, try dark shades of blue, like navy and midnight.

Are there specific colors that attract men and women?

Research has shown that women prefer soft colors and men prefer bright ones. Our totally unscientific experience has shown that boyfriends, husbands, fathers, and brothers delight when their formerly black-clothes-only gal puts on a feminine blouse in a color that flatters her.

ACKNOWLEDGMENTS

Thank you and thank you again Rebecca DiLiberto (Avant-Garde/Whimsical Moon) for your tireless work translating our Technicolor dreams into a literary reality.

Rita Wilson (Whimsical/Chic/Rocked-Out Earth) generously contributed her time and wit in writing the foreword—no small feat as she was simultaneously acting in one film and producing another, as well as contributing to her community, and serving as inspiration to women and mothers everywhere.

Our Visual Therapy team supported us completely and made this book happen: Lisa Marie McComb (Chic/Whimsical/Bohemian Earth) is our genius visual therapist, executive producer, and literal magic maker—oh, and she moonlights as a supermodel. Sarah Davidzuk (Chic/Avant-Garde Earth), Rory Michaels (Whimsical Star), Michael Kramer (Bohemian/Chic Earth), Kristi Porcelli (Chic/Whimsical Star) and Holly Jovenal (Bohemain/Earth) filled needs we didn't even know we had, from finding the perfect look for every shot, to helping create the global brand we're proud to call Visual Therapy.

Makeup guru Darcy McGrath (Chic Star) painted every gorgeous face you see in this book, and provided the two of us with endless touch-ups as well. Most important, she touched the heart of everyone on set. Darcy, thank you for your talent and laughter.

The pages of this book would be blank without the genius of our fabulous photographers: Michael Dar (Bohemian/Chic Sun) for fashion; Thomas Marlow (Bohemian Earth) and Mary Henebry (Bohemian/Chic Earth) for beauty.

Andy McNicol (Chic/Whimsical Earth) and our team at William Morris continue to make our dreams come true.

We are also grateful to:
Jane Stewart and Stephen Hall from Elite Chicago
Todd Okerstrom and Tina Sussman from Bergdorf Goodman
Decades
Tracey Smith of Lavande
Angel Sanchez
Christopher Coleman
Amy Fine Collins
Tracey Kemble
Lisa Perry
Patrick McDonald
Peter Gogarty
Bob Kowalski

Most importantly, thank you to our loving families who are our rock and our foundation, and all the dear friends who have supported us through this wonderful journey.

Jesse and Joe

CREDITS

INDEX

SUN

From peach to lemon, strawberry to mango, and lime to blueberry, shades on the sun palette are as refreshing as summer sorbet. Suns are golden girls—so they can wear tropical colors all year-round.

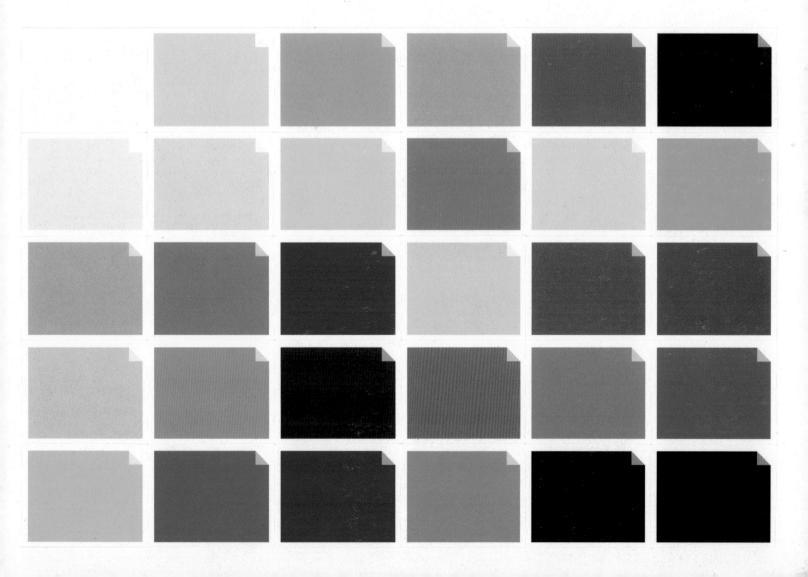